Evangelism has gone spiritual. Outsiders to the church no longer listen their way into the faith—they observe their way into faith and followership of Jesus. In *Jesus in the Mirror,* Tri and Jason capture one of the most effective ways to share one's faith in our present world: Reflect the heart of Christ in the way you live your life and invite others to a front-row seat of your own transformation.

Todd Hunter
Bishop of the Anglican Church in North America
Author of *The Outsider Interviews*

Even though the practice of evangelism has gone dark for most Christians, Tri and Jason bring us back to the core of what Jesus came to do. *Jesus in the Mirror* will transform the way you approach sharing your faith. It's not just about what you say or how you say it, but how authentically you live what you believe.

Gabe Lyons
Author of *The Next Christians* and Co-author of *UnChristian*
Founder of Q

I absolutely loved this book! A lot has been written concerning "missional" this and that—and this book goes beyond the read-but-don't-do missional stuff. Tri and Jason come at this from new angles that I found refreshing and encouraging. It's difficult to deposit hope in readers through the pages of a book, but they pulled it off. Buy this book and watch out—you just might end up becoming a dangerous person in Jesus' name!

Steve Sjogren
Author and Outreach Guru
www.ServeCoach.com

JESUS IN THE MIRROR

TRI ROBINSON
& JASON CHATRAW

Regal

For more information and
special offers from Regal Books, email us at
subscribe@regalbooks.com

Published by Regal
From Gospel Light
Ventura, California, U.S.A.
www.regalbooks.com
Printed in the U.S.A.

Published in association with the literary agency of D.J. Jacobson and Associates.
Agent: David Van Diest, 3689 Carman Drive, Suite 300, Los Oswego, OR 97035.

Library of Congress Cataloging-in-Publication Data
Robinson, Tri, 1948-
Jesus in the mirror : living a life that truly reflects him /
Tri Robinson & Jason Chatraw.
p. cm.
Includes bibliographical references and index.
ISBN 978-0-8307-6251-4 (trade paper : alk. paper)
1. Christian life. 2. Jesus Christ—Example. I. Chatraw, Jason. II. Title.
BV4501.3.R6428 2012
248.4—dc23
2012006089

Rights for publishing this book outside the U.S.A. or in non-English languages are
administered by Gospel Light Worldwide, an international not-for-profit ministry.
For additional information, please visit www.glww.org, email info@glww.org,
or write to Gospel Light Worldwide, 1957 Eastman Avenue, Ventura, CA 93003, U.S.A.

To order copies of this book and other Regal products in bulk quantities,
please contact us at 1-800-446-7735.

For the people who want to reflect Jesus more clearly.
May this book inspire you to reflect Him more each day.

CONTENTS

CONTENTS

ACKNOWLEDGMENTS

When the seed of an idea becomes a book, there are plenty of people to thank and acknowledge for their roles in seeing it come to fruition.

For starters, Steve Sjogren sparked this idea when he decided to go around Tampa wearing a "Please Forgive Steve" shirt. His ingenuity and creative gifts to the Church at large regarding outreach and how we think about sharing our faith have been invaluable, particularly to us personally.

We also appreciate Gabe Lyons's friendship and the way he has helped stir these conversations through the Q community. Gabe and Dave Kinnaman's book *UnChristian* provoked us to look further at the issue of evangelism and helped create a foundation for our thoughts on a new way forward when it comes to what is important as we share our faith.

Jim Henderson and Todd Hunter are also among those people in our lives who continually inspire us to examine and re-examine how we can be effective in reaching our culture with the transformative message of the gospel.

We would also like to thank David Van Diest and D.C. Jacobson & Associates for helping this project find a home—and Steve Lawson and Regal Books for believing that this idea might have some real value in the conversation on evangelism in the Church today.

Without these people and countless others we don't have the space to name, these ideas would never have the ability to take flight and, we hope, inspire Christians to become effective conduits of the gospel.

INTRODUCTION

After sitting through two days of hearing experts dissect the best way to share the gospel with others, I (Tri) was disappointed. None of the "tactics" shared in various workshops and plenary sessions made sense to me. Handing people a slick printed piece of information that succinctly divulged the gospel's narrative didn't seem like an effective process. Neither did just being good friends with someone and waiting for the moment when he or she just might ask me a question about God. While being at opposite ends of the spectrum, neither idea stirred me to go share my faith.

The greater question might be, "Why does anyone need to be stirred to go share his or her faith with others?" Shouldn't it be natural for those of us who believe in Christ to tell others about Him? We don't need to approach evangelism with guns blazing for the gospel, nor do we need to walk on eggshells lest we offend someone. There has to be a healthy middle ground.

That's what *Jesus in the Mirror* is all about—finding that empowering place where we don't feel guilty for speaking openly about Jesus or fearful that we're not really passionate about our faith if we fail to say "Jesus" every seventh word out of our mouths. We don't have all the answers but we are growing in our relationship with God each day and seeking to reflect Him more clearly.

On the way home from this particular conference, Jason and I found ourselves stuck in the San Francisco airport on a layover, chewing on what we had learned and what we intended to share with others. We both felt like something was missing from the approaches presented. Our concern had to do with our shared belief that evangelism is less about what you say and more about who you are. That was the crux of the matter.

As we talked, we used the tapestry on which so many ideas have been born—a napkin—to outline what we perceived as hindrances to sharing one's faith. Then we discussed the reasons people wouldn't receive what Christians had to say anyway. That list grew rather lengthy. After a while, we stopped adding to it. Dave Kinnaman and Gabe Lyons had already done a pretty good job, in their book *UnChristian*, of explaining why Christians were running uphill in sharing their faith.

Lyons and Kinnaman outlined how Christians are perceived by unbelievers—and their findings are haunting. Among many unflattering perceptions, non-Christians see Christians as **J**udgmental, **A**rrogant, **M**ean-spirited, **E**xclusive and **S**elf-righteous. Using these five traits, we created the acronym J.A.M.E.S. to refer to the "Christians" who leave such a lasting negative impression on those around them. Unfortunately, that's the image most of the world has attached to the word "Christian." Instead of seeing Jesus—who even reasonable atheists will admit had teachings that could change the world if everyone actually applied them—they see J.A.M.E.S. It repulses them. Non-believers wonder, *Why are Christians so indignant? Why won't they accept me? Why are they so judgmental? Why are they so unkind?* They're right to ask these questions.

Erwin McManus likes to say, "We're all hypocrites in transition." And he's got a point. There has to be room for grace as we stumble along this journey of experiencing the transformational power of the gospel. However, unbelievers aren't inclined to heap grace on those who claim to be righteous. They don't stick around long enough to witness the transition. Instead, they see the judgmental heart and the hypocrisy. Ultimately, they stop looking because they don't see Jesus. When Christians are judgmental, they're doing the same thing: refusing to believe that God can change a heart. However, it's more than being judgmental—it's an egregious misinterpretation of the gospel. If we don't believe God can change a person's life, what's the point?

Two things struck me as I reflected on *UnChristian* and this evangelism conference. The first was how important evangelism is to Christians. There are plenty of conferences designed around evangelism, focusing on how to share your faith and present a convincing argument for what you believe. Many of the ideas proffered place more value on your intellectual wit and gimmicks than on demonstrating how to live a life that displays authentic Christianity. They sound good in theory, but in practice, they fall flat. Christians definitely need to know what they believe and be able to articulate it in a winsome and convincing fashion—but that's different from making a person feel foolish or inadequate because they don't believe what you believe.

A "one-upmanship" approach to evangelism isn't about discipleship, which is the true calling of followers of Jesus. You don't make disciples simply by convincing someone to say a quick prayer, no matter how heartfelt it might be. Each person who initiates a relationship with Jesus needs to be encouraged, nurtured and taught about what it means to follow Him. Presenting the tenets of the gospel is merely the first step in the lifelong process that true evangelism should really be about.

In *UnChristian*, the authors share survey data indicating that traditional evangelism (making a case for faith in Jesus and attempting to get someone to pray "the sinner's prayer") makes people feel unimportant, like they were merely a project for a Christian portfolio. Kinnaman and Lyons write,

> Rather than being genuinely interested in people for their friendship, we often seem like spiritual headhunters.

Many of the young people we interviewed also pointed out how hard it is to take Christians seriously in light of some of their tactics. In all of the interviews we did, we heard no favorable comments about so-called street witnessing, where Christians intercept unknown passers-by to share the Good News. "People stalk you and verbally berate you. I'm like do I know you? Why should I care what you are saying?" was one comment. And outsiders expressed particular disdain for methods that "trick" people into paying attention. One respondent called this the "con of conversion."[1]

The second thing that caught my attention in *UnChristian* was the importance Christians place on lifestyle, which was defined as "doing the right thing, being good, not sinning."[2] This is where we've gone wrong in the Church. Our lifestyles are reflections of what we really believe, not what we say we believe. If we say we believe that knowing God's Word is of utmost importance, but we only read it twice a week, we don't really *believe* that God's Word is that important. We *think* it's important, but our actions belie our words. If we say we believe that prayer changes things, yet we don't pray much, we don't really believe in the power of prayer.

Ultimately, aligning our words with our actions is what the discipleship process is all about. It's about convincing our hearts that what Jesus said is true in a way that our heads also believe it. Once that happens, we can process all our actions and decisions through a grid that reflects a more accurate picture of the heart of Christ.

In between swapping stories and stalking Arianna Huffington down Concourse C (more on that in a moment), Jason and I filled up more than one napkin brainstorming what it would take to inspire and encourage the church I pastored in Boise to become the antidote to a widespread epidemic. We discussed what it would take to help people be "anti-evangelists"— not people who were determined to share their faith whether you wanted to hear it or not, but people whose lives simply oozed Jesus. I've found that when Jesus is flowing out of my life naturally, sharing my faith is effortless. I don't have to wring my hands over whether my friend is going to want to hear what I have to say regarding my faith. I don't have to worry that I might offend someone when I do mention Jesus' name either. When I'm living out my beliefs each day and seeking to show others the love of Christ, the questions will come— and they'll come naturally. Our curious friends will ask leading questions, beginning an inquisition that will enable me to point them to God.

During our conversation in the airport restaurant, talking heads blared on the televisions overhead, dissecting the 2008 presidential election, which had transpired just a few days earlier. Pundits wanted to know why the evangelical vote seemed splintered—why so many young Christians were breaking from the evangelical candidate of choice to vote for someone who wasn't a Republican. They couldn't figure this one out. One of those people asking this question was Arianna Huffington.

At the time, I had seen her on television talk shows but wasn't yet aware of her massive influence through her website, the Huffington Post. Jason briefed me as we watched her saunter by the restaurant before deciding to chase her down the concourse. We finally cornered her.

I stood behind Jason while he boldly proclaimed that I knew all the answers to the questions she was asking. As she put her cell phone call on hold, Arianna smiled politely at us. I wondered if I could actually answer the questions she was

asking. *What was she asking?* She told us to email her and she
would get back with us—and she did.

What I didn't realize at the moment was that the questions
she—and many other pundits—was asking could be answered
by the solution Jason and I had been discussing when it came
to evangelism. *Why were young adult Christians not voting for a Republican, in lockstep with the long-standing steadfast voting bloc?* For
the same reasons unbelievers didn't want to hear Christians
deliver a four-point treatise on the gospel: The person didn't
seem authentic in the way he or she lived out his or her faith.
The younger generation cares about the poor. They care about
the earth they're going to have to live on long after I've been
buried under it. They care about eradicating diseases and getting people clean water. They care about stamping out social
diseases like human trafficking. These are all areas where the
Church is vigorously at work, and, in many cases, leading the
way. But sadly, "Christian" political policies didn't seem to line
up with biblical precedence. Whether the assessment was accurate or simply perceived, the outcome was the same. A culture
of distrust emerged—and the votes went elsewhere.

But that doesn't have to be the case when people are confronted with the truth of the gospel. They can still choose Jesus—if they see Him. That must be our goal when it comes to
sharing the gospel. We must make every effort to allow God's
transforming power to shape us more and more into the image of Christ. We want people to see Jesus when they look at
us. By that, I mean they should see a heart of compassion that
looks past all the junk in people's lives and sees who God created them to be—and then lovingly calls them to pursue Him.
Yet there are many obstacles to clear first.

One of the biggest obstacles is ourselves. We must face
the reality that we are hypocrites in a painstakingly slow tran-

sition—and that there are countless others like us, many of whom have hurt unbelievers. In fact, they just might be the reason that one of our friends has decided that following Jesus will never be for him or her. Who would want to join a group where hurtful and hypocritical people gather? What about my pain, my hurts?

Out of this daunting realization, we crafted a sermon series called "Please Forgive J.A.M.E.S." The messages were aimed at helping Christians understand how others perceive them. Sometimes the perceptions are accurate; other times, they are not. But because, in many respects, perception is reality, the results are the same: people avoid Jesus not because of Him but because of His followers. If anything, this perception of Christians serves as a reminder that we need to be extra vigilant to reflect the heart of Christ every moment. Failing to diligently reflect Jesus results in the world viewing Christians as Judgmental, Arrogant, Mean-spirited, Exclusive and Self-righteous, among many other things. So we encouraged our church members to ask their unbelieving friends for forgiveness on behalf of those Christians who had hurt them in the past. It was a way to disarm that hostility that has built up among non-believers who have been legitimately harmed by well-intentioned but, perhaps, misguided Christians.

I must warn you that this suggestion wasn't popular with everyone. I got nasty letters from people who defiantly questioned why they should ask for forgiveness for something they never did (never mind that Nehemiah and Jesus both did it). But that was the point. We wanted people to develop hearts of humility—hearts that resembled Jesus' nature. It wasn't about being right all the time—it was about accurately portraying Christ's heart for others. God's desire is that all may come to know Him.

Despite our best intentions as Christians, we don't always help accomplish that goal. Sometimes the world accurately perceives our misguided motives and brands Christians as vile and deceitful. Sometimes the world is dead on—and it's tough to hear the truth. However, hearing those hard truths is essential if we want to be authentic followers of Christ. Our "Please Forgive J.A.M.E.S." series helped us find some common language around the poor perception that the world has of Christians. It framed our idea of what we can become if we're not constantly holding up Jesus as the one whose life we desire to reflect.

Unfortunately, we watched people leave the church during this series. Many angrily told me they would never ask forgiveness for something they didn't do. It was disheartening. However, this series also brought new people *to* our church— people who walked in the door and said "thank you" for teaching our members how to represent Jesus in a way they could relate to.

As you begin reading this book, our hope is that you discover a new way to share your faith—a way that's less concerned with "gotcha" questions and more concerned with the heart of a person. We all have a lot room for growth when it comes to more clearly reflecting Jesus in our everyday lives. Nobody has it all figured out. It's definitely important to understand what you believe, and there are plenty of great books already written that address thought-provoking apologetics. But our aim here is something different: We want Christians to understand that as our own lives are transformed, we want to reflect all the great things about the character of Jesus, not the things that drive people away from the Church. We deeply love the Church with all her faults and unheralded successful ways she touches people. The culture of the Church is what we live and breathe. But we know most outsiders won't stick around long enough to see the good the incredible Body of Christ is doing if we behave in a way that dims that reflection of Jesus in our own lives. We believe that the more we grasp the ideas and principles laid out in these pages, the more we will become people who effortlessly share our faith. It won't be because we have learned an intricate system to mentally outwit those who have yet to begin following Jesus, but it will happen because we so reflect the heart of the One who is irresistible in the way that He loves.

Tri Robinson & Jason Chatraw • www.regalbooks.com

Part I

THE STATE OF OUR HEARTS

Chapter 1

A BROKEN HEART FOR A BROKEN WORLD

Let your religion be less of a theory and more of a love affair.

G. K. Chesterton

Have you ever met someone who changed your life? Someone whose mere presence shifted the direction of your journey? It could be someone you are grateful you met, or it could be someone you wish you had never encountered. But these people—whoever they are—serve as keystones in our journeys of faith.

Sometimes these same people instigate powerful moments—moments that not only redirect our paths but also bring definition to what we believe to be true. For me (Jason), one such person was Natalie.

When I met Natalie, my first instinct was to avoid her. She looked far too young to allow her body to serve as the well-decorated canvas that it was—and that disturbed me. Her impenetrable defensive posture was even more troubling to me. What was she guarding? She made no secret of how difficult her life was, and she often expressed how unhappy she was about that—but she didn't want to talk about it. Or at least, that's what I thought.

After a long day of work, the first thing I wanted to do was go inside and rest. I had no interest in pausing to listen to the rants of an angry 19-year-old girl. Undaunted, she would follow me up the steps leading to my apartment door, telling me fanciful stories that seemed more like fiction than fact. The more tales I heard, the more I realized what a twisted life she had. A mother who had abandoned her. An overbearing father who drank too much. No direction in life. Not even a dream. She even showed me her drug stash once. The whole situation was undeniably sad. But for some reason, she seemed dangerous to me, like she wanted to drag me into her world. I just thought it was best to stay away from her.

I had always considered myself a compassionate person. Whenever I saw the images of starving children in Africa on television, I wanted to pick up the phone and make a donation. If I heard about a need in church, I wanted to help. But when it came to a real live person, one I had to get down in the squalor with, I hesitated to get involved. I raised my guard around Natalie and tried not to dwell on it. Until one night.

Arriving home from a powerful evening worship service, I found Natalie sobbing on the steps. The rough exterior? Gone. The reality of her brokenness? Now a visible pile of shards. In that moment, my heart broke for Natalie. As she shared what had happened, I could actually feel her pain. Her boyfriend had dumped her, and her girlfriends had decided they wanted to go out partying rather than sit with Natalie in her depressed state to console her. She was alone. I sat with her for more than an hour, listening to her heartbreak.

Then I went inside and cried myself. What kind of person was I that I had wanted to avoid her? How could I have been so callous toward a broken person like Natalie? Why was I so arrogant and judgmental in the way I looked down upon her plight in life? That night, I began a journey of questioning my own heart—and demanding some answers regarding why I had been so resistant to let God soften my heart in this area. Surely, this wasn't who God wanted me to be. I was being a J.A.M.E.S. Christian. I was unwittingly embracing the way the world perceived Christians—acting as a judgmental, arrogant, mean-spirited, exclusive and self-righteous Christian. (If you missed the J.A.M.E.S. explanation in the introduction, do yourself a favor and go back to read it before you go any further.)

I began to ask God to break my heart for the broken. My prayers were radical. Whenever I identified an area of callousness in my heart, I asked God to work. As a "glass is half full" kind of guy, I had never understood how a person could just get depressed. After one of my friends shared that he was struggling with depression, I asked God to let me feel what my friend was feeling. The next morning while I was taking a shower, this overwhelming depression came over me. I wanted to go straight to bed and call my work and say I was sick. I felt strangely hopeless. It was the weirdest sensation; I could not explain it and certainly had never experienced anything like it before. Then I remembered my prayer. For the entire day, I felt a heavy depression. The next morning, it lifted—and I wept. *That's what it feels like to be depressed,* I thought. Today, I no longer issue a canned "cheer up" response when someone tells me they are depressed. I understand a bit of what they are going through.

After that pivotal night, my relationship with Natalie changed dramatically. Now, when I arrived home from work and found her sitting on the steps, I did not rush past her. Instead, I loosened my collar and tie and sat down to hear about her day. Teenage gossip. One friend stabbing another friend in the back. A lot of the news seemed petty, but to Natalie, it was important.

Then one day, she finally asked me about my job and what I did. At the time, I worked as a writer for a major Christian ministry magazine. I could have sidestepped the impending collision by simply telling her I was an assistant editor for a magazine, but where's the fun in that? So, I divulged all the details and braced for impact. The effect of my revelation was not at all what I had expected. Suddenly, our conversations shifted from "he said, she said" retellings to deep, probing discussions about faith and God and life. I realized Natalie had more questions than I had answers—and yet I was not discouraged about this. Natalie even began reading her Bible and would tell me about it sometimes. That was encouraging, to say the least.

Over the next few months, Natalie invited me into her life. I met boyfriends and girlfriends on a regular basis. Some were fixtures; others floated in and out of her life. Whenever I stopped to reflect on how the scene of me talking about life with a bunch of directionless teenagers must have looked to my neighbors, it made me smile. It was divine comedy—only God could create space for a well-dressed, professional-looking writer to hang out with a bunch of tattooed and pierced grunge teens. I learned about punk bands, got invited to raves, and increased my vocabulary with the new hip words of the moment. I watched as my heart began to swell for these broken teenagers.

When God initiates a transforming work in our hearts with our permission, the results are amazing—but sometimes it takes awhile for us to notice them. I knew God was breaking my heart for the broken world around me, but I didn't realize the full extent of it at first. Was I really falling in love with this broken world? My time with Christian friends rejuvenated me. My time with broken people still searching for God brought me closer to Him. I was beginning to understand His heart for this world. Jesus didn't just die for Christians—He died for *everyone*.

It might sound simplistic, and you may have grasped this a long time ago, but this concept was revolutionary for me. Everyone meant *everyone*. There wasn't a person in my life that Jesus didn't die for and desperately want to have a relationship with. Yet somehow, I had become smug in my faith—assured of my spiritual superiority because of how good I was. What I didn't understand was the full extent of God's love—and how my good behavior didn't impress Him when it came from a heart that felt duty-bound rather than overflowing with love. Up until that point, I had found fullness in my faith by how good I had become, only to dive into depths of despair when I willfully committed a sinful act. Grace was for those people who needed it, not for me. But now something was happening to me. As I was falling in love with a broken world, my own heart was changing.

One afternoon, I realized just how entrenched I had become in the lives of these teens who were seeking something to give them purpose in life. I stopped at the foot of the stairs to see Natalie and one of her friends, Stacy, sitting there with a new guy I had never met. We exchanged names before Stacy chimed in, "Jason's cool—he'll even remember your name!" I knew that people enjoy the sweet sound of their own name (when it's uttered for a positive reason), so I had always made an effort to remember people's names. With these teens, I made especially sure to remember their names because they had become important to me. However, I had no idea that practice would result in my being labeled as "cool" among them, nor did I realize just how much hearing their names meant to them.

Why did I remember their names? Why was Stacy so impressed by this fact? Pneumonic name tricks aside, I learned their names because I had begun to care about them. I listened to their hearts and then went and prayed for them. In reflecting on that moment, I realized God had broken my heart for these teenagers. No longer did I see them as directionless losers—I saw them as people God created and cherished. My heart had been broken and there was no going back.

Jerry and His Dog

I (Tri) gave my life to Christ in the heat of the Jesus Movement that so radically impacted the Baby Boomer generation throughout the 1970s. This movement, like many moves of God, was birthed out of a kind of rebellion. Our passion was fueled not only by our newfound faith in Jesus, but also in reaction to our past experiences with organized religion. We were the first to call seminary "cemetery," believing that we didn't need years of theological training to proclaim the words and do the works of Jesus. We believed that God could do extraordinary things with ordinary people—and we stood ready to prove it. Our young, radical preachers exhorted us, week after week, to get out into the streets and be the hands and feet of Jesus. They were full of passion, and we believed them as they constantly told stories of how God was using our generation to share the gospel with others in life-giving ways. We were motivated and eager, even though we were immature and scared to death.

I'll never forget hearing my pastor teach the familiar passage from Matthew 25 that describes how Jesus talked about separating the sheep from the goats:

> Then the righteous will answer him, "Lord, when did we see you hungry and feed you, or thirsty and give you something to drink? When did we see you a stranger

and invite you in, or needing clothes and clothe you? When did we see you sick or in prison and go to visit you?" The King will reply, "I tell you the truth, whatever you did for one of the least of these brothers of mine, you did for me" (Matt. 25:37-40).

My pastor exhorted us to lay down our insecurities and become obedient to Jesus' commission. With everything in me, I wanted to be bold. I desired to show the courage many of my contemporaries were demonstrating, but I worried that when the opportunity came I might fail. I was a secondary school teacher at the time, and I distinctly remember praying when I was alone in my classroom one day for an opportunity to exercise my faith. I asked God to give me an encounter with someone who needed a touch from Him.

When I left the house that morning for work, my wife, Nancy, had given me a list of things she needed for the discipleship group that would be meeting in our home that evening. She asked if I would stop at the market on my way home (a common occurrence since we lived an hour outside of town).

After school I stopped at the market, parked the car, and headed at a brisk pace for the store's doors. I was a man on a mission, wanting to get what I needed so that I could make it home in plenty of time to eat before our meeting. The thought of what I had prayed for earlier that day was gone from my mind. In fact, I didn't even recall it as I spotted someone I presumed to be a street person sitting next to a broken, dilapidated bicycle beside the doors. He honestly was one of the most "downtrodden" people I had ever seen in our small town. He looked sad and lost as he fumbled through his dirty pack. He glanced up as I walked by, and our eyes momentarily connected. I didn't know what to say but felt the need to say something. The words, "Hi, how are you doing?" found their way out of my mouth.

His simple response was, "Not so good."

"Oh," I said and walked on by and into the store.

I made it all the way to the aisle where I was to pick up the assigned goods before I began to feel convicted by the Holy Spirit. It felt like a sharp stick. God poked and prodded me, reminding me of the prayer I had prayed. I knew I had failed and was angry with myself. I had to do something, say something more meaningful—anything but walk on by in a state of indifference. I felt foolish and sheepish as I dropped what I was doing and headed back for the doors. I walked through them and was relieved to see the man still there. I asked again, "How are you doing?"

His response was similar to his first when he said, "Not very well."

I then said, "I'm sorry to hear that" and once again kept on walking. I arrived at my car, feeling like a complete loser. I knew I was a spiritual weakling with a backbone as firm as a wet noodle. Not only had I failed the Lord, but also I had failed Nancy. I hadn't picked up her things and couldn't bear the thought of walking by this poor guy again. I thought about driving across town to another store, but decided it might be better to give prayer another try instead. I did, and again the Lord convicted me to take courage and go back. I slowly opened my car door and walked up to the young man for the third time. I asked him if he was hungry, and he replied that he was. I told him that if he would stay where he was, I would be right back after I picked up a few things for my wife. When I finished my shopping and came back outside, I was glad to see that he hadn't moved.

I had thought about buying him something to eat while I was in this large convenience store and simply handing it to him, but the Lord put it on my heart to be bolder than that. I wasn't exactly truthful when I told him I was about to get something to eat for myself, especially in light of the fact that I had a Bible study to get to. I asked him if he would join me for dinner. He was visibly surprised by the offer, but said with a bit of caution in his voice that he would. There was a fast food place a few blocks away, and I suggested we meet there, since it appeared everything he owned was tied to his bicycle. In a few minutes, he showed up and we ordered. We found an empty table and sat down together.

During the next hour, I got to know Jerry. I learned about his broken life and how he ended up on the street. I also learned why this particular day had been one of the worst in his life. He shared with me that several years earlier he had found a small stray dog that had become the only real friend he had ever had. They had spent every day together. The dog just sat on the back of Jerry's bike, perched on his pack, as they traveled from place to place.

Sadly, that very day the dog, Jerry's best and only friend in the world, had fallen off the bike into traffic and been killed by a passing car. We actually cried together as God exposed His heart for this perfect stranger to me. I knew that what happened between Jerry and me that afternoon was not an accident, but an answer to my prayer. I had sincerely asked God to give me not only a heart for broken people, but also the courage to reach out in compassion and mercy on His behalf. I had nearly missed the blessing.

Surprisingly, I wasn't even late for our discipleship home group that night; and Nancy wasn't upset when I told her why I wasn't hungry for the dinner she had prepared. I had experienced God's grace at work, and the lessons I learned that day were powerful and life changing.

A few years later, I entered full-time ministry. I've now been serving the Lord in this capacity for nearly 30 years, always trying to encourage others to rise above their inadequacies and obey God's commission to minister to the downtrodden. My experience with Jerry all those years ago has never left me. It's made me aware that each of us must muster the courage to move beyond our insecurities and leave our comfort zones in order to reach out and touch the lives of a broken society around us. It has taught me that until we have experienced and even touched God's heart for this broken world, our actions will be mechanical—merely going through the motions of ministry—and the words we speak will be empty. God has called us to be a people of authenticity and sincerity in all we do. This will only happen when we can see our own weaknesses and are trusting enough to say "yes" in obedience to His call.

We're All Broken

When we speak of "this broken world," it's not as if we aren't part of it. We're all broken on some level or another, dealing with our insecurities, weaknesses and foibles. We struggle to allow the Holy Spirit to renew our minds daily and to walk out the gospel in a way that honors God. But for some reason, we like to rank our Christianity by comparing ourselves to others. When we take inventory of our brokenness, we tend to frame it in the context of others. *At least I don't have that guy's problem*, we might think to ourselves. *I may have some struggles, but I'm much more faithful than she is*, we could say. Why do we make others our standard for determining that our brokenness doesn't matter as much?

When I (Jason) play golf, I have to control my competitive desire to score better than the other players who are with me. If I'm playing with some hacks like myself, it's easy for me to drift into this mentality where I check everyone's scorecard after each hole and keep a rigid count in my head of how many strokes each person has made. I want to be the best hack out there. However, if I am playing with more experienced golfers, I tend to ignore what each person scores, as I know I will never measure up. Instead, I focus on doing little things to improve my golf game—not because I want to win, but because I want to do better. Oddly enough, when I'm not trying to compete with everyone else, I usually end up with a better score and not everyone thinks I'm a hack (my father-in-law excepted—he *knows* I'm a hack).

As Christians, we must understand that Christianity isn't about a race to heaven; it's about a journey that leads us to a place of deeper realization of who God is, how much He loves us, and what He wants to do with our lives. There is also no shame in being broken; it's just what we are. God desires to take that brokenness and weave it into a beautiful tapestry that we never could have imagined. He takes our broken pieces and reforms them, allowing us to become part of His greater plan. It's not about an individual expression of our faith, but about playing a pivotal role in God's plan of redemption—for *everyone*.

Jesus lived in the midst of broken people. He didn't see these shattered souls as the pariahs that the rest of the culture saw them as. Paralytic, deaf, mute—it didn't matter to Jesus. He saw them all the same. He saw them as the broken people they were. He saw them as people whom God wanted to make whole again.

We can devise the most convincing arguments about God and His existence to present to an unbelieving world, but nothing compares to the testimony of one broken person becoming whole again. Jesus consistently spent time with the downtrodden and broken. Take note of this account, found in Matthew 9, of what happened following His interactions with them:

> When Jesus entered the ruler's house and saw the flute
> players and the noisy crowd, he said, "Go away. The
> girl is not dead but asleep." But they laughed at him.
> After the crowd had been put outside, he went in and
> took the girl by the hand, and she got up. News of this
> spread through all that region.
>
> As Jesus went on from there, two blind men followed him, calling out, "Have mercy on us, Son of
> David!"
>
> When he had gone indoors, the blind men came
> to him, and he asked them, "Do you believe that I am
> able to do this?"
>
> "Yes, Lord," they replied.
>
> Then he touched their eyes and said, "According to
> your faith will it be done to you"; and their sight was restored. Jesus warned them sternly, "See that no one
> knows about this." But they went out and spread the
> news about him all over that region (Matt. 9:23-31).

*News of this spread through all that region . . . But they went out
and spread the news about him all over that region.* These people
couldn't keep quiet about Jesus—even when He told them to
tell no one. *I just saw a dead girl walk out of her room, so, sure, I'll
keep that to myself, Jesus.* Broken people were being put back together again. This was big news. Broken things don't fix themselves, and everyone knew it.

To become broken for a broken world is to never forget the
broken state in which you came to Christ. No matter how long

ago it was, the moment you met Christ was the moment He began to put you back together. It's a work begun by God, not by us. In our arrogance, we think we had something to do with it. The attitude of J.A.M.E.S. begins to creep upon us. *We deserve this, right?* On one level, we did have *something* to do with this work God began in us—we chose to accept God's love and follow Him. But that merely provided an opportunity for God to do a supernatural work in our lives to restore us and make us pliable to be used for His good purposes. What we did was significant and insignificant at the same time. We cranked the car, but someone else bought it, gassed it up for us, stepped on the accelerator, and began driving. Yet we somehow forget all that if we're not mindful of God's great love for us—and how He wants us to have that same heart for others.

In order for us to share the powerful redemptive work God has done in our own lives and reflect the heart of Jesus, we have to remember the places from which we came. We didn't know all the answers. We were far from perfect, with years and years of work to be done. If we're honest with ourselves, we can even acknowledge that no matter how long we've been following Jesus, there remains more work to be done in our hearts.

In 1 Corinthians 6, the apostle Paul goes into detail about the darkness that was in people's souls before they met Christ—before their lives were radically changed. He writes, "But you were washed, you were sanctified, you were justified in the name of the Lord Jesus Christ and by the Spirit of our God" (1 Cor. 6:11). David E. Garland interprets Paul's words like this: "God's grace does not mean that God benignly accepts humans in all their fallenness, forgives them, and then leaves them in that fallenness. God is in the business not of whitewashing sins but of transforming sinners."[1]

It's this misunderstanding of God's purpose for grace in our lives that often sends us down the wrong path in the name of evangelism. We mistakenly believe that the moment we begin to follow Christ, we have reached the zenith of our spiritual journey on earth: "We're going to heaven." Sure, we believe God is going to change us and transform us and help us be better people . . . but we're going to heaven! And that becomes the name of the game. Convince someone to say the sinner's prayer and we've scored a heavenly touchdown. But that perspective on what it means to become a Christian cheapens the sacrifice Jesus made. God's grace is infinitely deeper and far more powerful than we realize—and until we do realize it, we're stuck believing a toothless gospel, one that saves but doesn't transform.

In his book *Transforming Grace*, Jerry Bridges explains the power and purpose of God's grace:

> This is the amazing story of God's grace. God saves us by His grace and transforms us more and more into the likeness of His Son by His grace. In all our trials and afflictions, He sustains and strengthens us by His grace. He calls us by grace to perform our own unique function within the body of Christ. Then, again by grace, He gives to each of us the spiritual gifts necessary to fulfill our calling. As we serve Him, He makes that service acceptable to Himself by grace, and then rewards us a hundredfold by grace.[2]

Our hearts become broken when we humbly realize that we're all the same in the journey of life. We want significance and purpose. Most of all, we want to be whole. We tire of experiencing a life that always seems like something is missing.

It isn't until we discover the love of Christ that we begin to catch glimpses of life the way God intended it to be. Pure joy. Relentless love. Overwhelming forgiveness. Intimate relationship. It's what we always dreamed of—and we want others to experience it as well. But they'll never believe or hear us if we haven't allowed God to do the deep redemptive work in our own lives that is necessary to put us on a path to wholeness.

Having a broken heart for a broken world means we recognize that without God's grace, we might still be mired in our own brokenness. When we see others in that light—understanding that they, too, need to see people being the hands and feet of Jesus in their lives—we can look at them with the eyes of Jesus. We not only see their broken circumstances but can also be part of God's plan to restore them.

But that can only happen if we live like Jesus, committing ourselves to becoming more like Him and less like J.A.M.E.S. Before we can do that, we need to understand who J.A.M.E.S. is and how we can be diligent to reflect the heart of Jesus instead of projecting the glaring faults of J.A.M.E.S.

Part II

DISCOVERING
HIS HEART

Chapter 2

THE VERDICT ON JUDGMENTAL CHRISTIANS

Judgmental → Patient

*One of the great disadvantages of hurry is
that it takes such a long time.*
G. K. Chesterton

Playing the role of judge is a favorite pastime in our culture. It doesn't even matter what the subject is, because we're ready to judge anything. Pundits judge Hollywood stars for their attire on the red carpet, telling us who was the worst and best dressed of the event. Websites allow us to upload photos of ourselves and have anonymous people judge our looks. We judge books—some by their content, some by their covers. We judge restaurants. We judge college football teams. We judge our friends' Facebook posts with "likes." We judge websites that judge websites. We live in a culture that is obsessed with judging things.

Yet we all cringe when we are deemed a judgmental Christian by someone. We refuse to condone a certain behavior or mindset that is accepted by our collective society, and suddenly we're cast as *that* person—the person who thinks he or she is morally superior to everyone. The truth is that we just might be judgmental in our hearts. Or we could be completely innocent of the accusation, simply exercising wisdom and employing biblical support as we cautiously assess a situation. Sometimes the perception arises from confusion surrounding the word "judgmental" and what it actually means in each situation. Other times the reality is more uncomfortable; sometimes we are truly embracing a judgmental spirit that is destructive and at odds with the way Jesus lived.

UnChristian authors Gabe Lyons and Dave Kinnaman address how strongly unbelievers feel about the judgmental spirit of Christians, writing, "One of outsiders' most significant concerns about present-day Christianity: Christians are judgmental. Respondents to our surveys believe Christians are trying, consciously or not, to justify feelings of moral and spiritual superiority."[1] Similarly, "Outsiders think of Christians as quick to judge others. They say we are not honest about our attitudes and perspectives about other people. They doubt that we really love people as we say we do."[2]

To accuse someone of being judgmental has strong negative connotations in our society—despite the fact that we love to judge things. It's easy to conclude that what people really mean is this: When *you* judge *me*, I am offended. People neither want you to disapprove of their behavior, nor do they want to be held accountable for their actions. This pervasive attitude in our culture has rendered traditional evangelism techniques null and void for all intents and purposes. People are quick to put up defenses when they sense your disapproval about the way they are living. While we must be aware that this is how nonbelievers tend to respond to a judgmental approach to sharing the gospel, it is also helpful to understand what Jesus meant when He talked about judging others.

There were moments in Jesus' teaching when, on the surface, He seemed to contradict Himself. For instance, there's some well-founded concern and confusion when it comes to understanding what Jesus meant when talking about judging. Just take a moment to contemplate the following two verses:

> Stop judging by mere appearances, and make a right judgment (John 7:24).

> Do not judge, or you too will be judged. For in the same way you judge others, you will be judged, and with the measure you use, it will be measured to you (Matt. 7:1-2).

In the verse from the book of John, Jesus instructs His followers to quit judging based solely upon what we see and hear. There is always much more to the story—much more to a person's heart than physical circumstances that are common knowledge. We could be right, but can we really be sure? If we are sure, it's likely that we are friends of the person in question, and that any judgment we might make would come in the form of a gentle rebuke wrapped up with love and encouragement. That's judging correctly.

In the verse in Matthew, Jesus recognizes that a culture of being judgmental toward others takes its toll. Are you harsh in your judgment of others? Or are you fair? Do you want others to be fair with you?

Christians begin to invoke the spirit of J.A.M.E.S. when they cling to John 7 as their divine right to judge others. But as Jesus so often does during His teaching, He calls for restraint—for a proper perspective. Only God can see into the hearts of human beings, yet we act as if we have this ability when we jump up on the judgment seat and bang a gavel in condemnation of an unsuspecting person.

On Jesus' instruction that we "make a right judgment," F. B. Meyer writes this:

> There is abundant need for a right and sound judgment, illuminated by the Spirit of truth; but there is a world of difference between it and the censorious and critical opinions, which we are apt to form and utter about others. Human nature is fond of climbing up into the judgment-seat and proclaiming its decisions without hearing both sides or calling witnesses. Beware of basing your judgment on idle stories and gossip. In any case, do not utter it if it be adverse unless you have first prayed about it and sought to turn the sinner from the error of his ways. Let God search you before you search another.

The apostle Paul seeks to bring clarification to the issue of judgment, explaining that we need to be a good judge of our fellow Christians—and leave the world alone:

> What business is it of mine to judge those outside the church? Are you not to judge those inside? God will judge those outside. "Expel the wicked man from among you" (1 Cor. 5:12-13).

If others are to see Jesus in our lives, we won't reflect a condemning spirit. There will always be those who take issue with what the Bible says. They will either thumb their noses at the Word and call the Bible outdated or they will bend and twist the text to justify their stances or behavior. But no matter how adverse people might be to what the Bible says, Christians who desire to reflect Jesus should remember that we're called to treat others with love and grace. Some unbelievers may not accept Jesus because they don't want to change the way they are living. But they should never reject Jesus because of the way we share the message.

The Anti-Judgment

When we address the judgmental spirit in our own lives, there is one glaring prescription: Be more grace-filled. Grace clearly overcomes a judgmental spirit, as pronouncements of guilt are replaced by unmerited favor or unconditional love or sincere acceptance. A judgmental attitude doesn't stand a chance when held up to the light of God's grace. We'll talk more about grace later in this book, because in this chapter we want to address a less obvious antidote to a judgmental heart: patience.

Life would look quite different if there were no time. We would not be constrained by a clock that starts ticking down from the minute we are born. The continuum in which we live would offer us a great expanse from which to work. Nothing would be last minute, because we would have infinite minutes. "Urgency" would not be part of our vocabulary. Why do today what you have forever to do? We might not even know what "today" means.

But we have no such luxury. Time is of the essence with most things that we do. It drives us to accomplish things, get to places and help others. It governs our life like a benevolent dictator—and sometimes like a malevolent one. So, we bow down to its rushing and urgency. We cannot escape its powerful grip.

While God sees our lives in light of eternity, we do not. We see life in a very fixed timeframe. That timeframe may be shorter than we would prefer, but it's not like we have a choice. In order for us to capture God's heart for others, we must see the world as He sees it, realizing that even though our time here is short, it's not necessary to rush through it—or rush others.

Much of our judgmental spirit has to do with the fact that we have deemed others to be "out of time." We don't see how they are going to change—not in this lifetime, anyway. It's over for them. There is no chance for restitution or repentance—no opportunity to turn their lives around. This is it. Final. Done. Judged.

Yet God views our lives differently. He sees the hope—the promise. He recognizes those gifts He placed within us and knows they will soon blossom. It's far too early for judgment, because plenty of time remains. He knows how the 45-year-old man we think will never accept Jesus will become undone at age 70. He knows that the hard-hearted 15-year-old boy who causes problems at school will become a powerful evangelist in another 15 years. He knows that the 16-year-old girl who just aborted her baby will begin spending the rest of her life speaking out for the voiceless once she turns 20.

We see those people as a lost cause. They're done. We've judged them as degenerates, losers and rebellious sinners. We assume they are beyond hope and leave them for dead.

Yet those are exactly the kind of people Jesus interacted with while He was on earth—the kind of people He came to save.

While Jesus was having dinner at Levi's house, many tax collectors and "sinners" were eating with him and his disciples, for there were many who followed him. When the teachers of the law who were Pharisees saw him eating with the "sinners" and tax collectors, they asked his disciples: "Why does he eat with tax collectors and 'sinners'?" On hearing this, Jesus said to them, "It is not the healthy who need a doctor, but the sick. I have not come to call the righteous, but sinners" (Mark 2:15-17).

When we condemn someone as a sinner, what we are really saying is that they are beyond help. We don't think they will ever turn their lives around. So, we walk away. But not Jesus. Those were the very people He zeroed in on—His number one target. Those were the people who *needed* Him. Forget timeframes and deadlines. This was a battle for souls, and Jesus was going to win with His patient approach. He could wait out the course evil was going to take in someone's life with love and grace. His refusal to pronounce judgment provided time for a person to experience the gospel's life-changing power.

We don't usually have a problem with patience for ourselves. We readily acknowledge that God is still working on us. When it comes to our own sin, grace flows like a fountain. It's just that other people need to have their stuff together—yesterday. Their sinful nature cramps our style and prevents us from reflecting Jesus.

The German monk Thomas à Kempis reminds us of this contradiction by poking a little fun at the unrealistic demands we sometimes place on others:

> Endeavor to be always patient of the faults and imperfections of others; for thou hast many faults and imperfections of thine own that require forbearance. If thou art not able to make thyself that which thou wishest, how canst thou expect to mold another in conformity to thy will?

Jesus never rushed anywhere, even when those around Him deemed the situation urgent. He knew what He was doing and who was in control. Instead of living in a state of panic, He exuded peace by the way He handled Himself in every situation—even in the most dire ones.

The apostle Paul teaches us that patience is a virtue of love—the Christlike love that we're charged with demonstrating for the world (see 1 Cor. 13:4). Patience allows time and space for God's deep love to soak into the dry ground of a resistant heart. Despite the pressure to rush or act, patience relaxes, trusting that God is at work even when we can't see Him doing what we want Him to do when we want Him to do it.

Jesus talked about urgency within God's kingdom, but He didn't coerce people to experience Him. *You'd better call for Me to come heal you, because you never know if I'll be around again to help you pick up that mat and go home.* Jesus didn't work that way, because He knew that God was already at work in the lives of those He met. Even the patience Jesus demonstrated during His time on earth was miniscule compared to the patience God has for humanity. A good thing came to the One who waited—the opportunity to reconcile the world with Father God.

Never Too Far Gone

In our effort to share our faith with others, it's easy to write off some of the people we encounter immediately. But that's not what Jesus did. If we intend to reflect the heart of Jesus to the world, we must understand that He hasn't given up on any of us. Our well of optimism is practically dry in comparison to God's. He waits out our rebellion and disobedience in the hope that we will return to Him.

While Nancy and I (Tri) were still living in our little valley just outside of Boise, Nancy read a passage out of the book of Deuteronomy one morning in her devotions. We had been thinking about selling our home and moving farther away from the city, but as of yet we hadn't found the right place. The passage she read included Deuteronomy 1:6-8, which provides an account of how God spoke through Moses, telling the people of Israel that they had stayed in the place they were long enough, and it was time to pull up their tent pegs and advance into the hill country He had prepared for them. After praying about what she had just read, Nancy excitedly called me to tell me that she felt God had prepared a place in the hills for us to relocate. The next week, she saw a small add in a local throwaway paper that advertised 80 acres in the hills an hour outside of Boise. I wasn't too interested, but because she believed God was going to lead us to a special place in the hill country, she called and set up an appointment to see the property the next day. That's how we met Brian.

The first time I saw Brian was at our meeting place at a one-lane bridge that crossed the Payette River. The narrow bridge gave access to a dirt road that ascended the side of a steep, rugged canyon. Right away I knew Brian was different somehow. He wore khaki shorts, hiking boots and a cowboy hat. By the brown color of his weathered skin, it was obvious to us that he was a person who had spent a good deal of time in the outdoors. We shook hands briefly and were instructed to follow his one-ton, dual four-wheeled diesel truck up the narrow mountain road. As we climbed, the road grew steeper, dropping off on our left-hand side hundreds of feet into the canyon below. I watched as Nancy's knuckles gripped the dash and thought to myself that the journey up the mountain would likely convince her she had somehow missed hearing the Lord's voice accurately.

The road climbed and wound up the canyon for some five miles until we broke out on top in high, open, rolling terrain—and everything changed. We could see in every direction, and the panoramic view was captivating. In the distance before us stood an unusual looking mountain that at first glance had the appearance of a small volcano, except for the large stand of timber across its crest. Its rounded sides were covered with grass that waved and changed color in the afternoon breeze, catching my eye as well as my imagination. This was Timber Butte, though at that point we didn't know its name. It was hill country more than mountainous—cattle country that had been homesteaded years before. Here and there, small farmhouses, barns and fences that obviously hadn't been occupied or used for years remained. In the distance to the north and east, forested mountains still held onto the last of the winter snow. From that moment, we were smitten by a country that, just a few minutes earlier, we didn't even know existed.

We followed Brian right to the bottom of Timber Butte, where he stopped his truck and got out. We followed his lead and stepped out into the cool fresh air and invigorating smells of spring. Everything was green, and I told Nancy later that I had fully expected Julie Andrews to come prancing over the hill, singing. In my unbelief, I never dreamed this would one day be our home.

With Brian, we walked the land from one end to the other, and we knew then that—with God's provision—we would one day want to own it. After returning to our vehicles, Brian gave us his price. We in turn told him that if our home sold before he found another buyer, we would make him an offer. We thanked him for taking the time to meet us, and then we spent the next few minutes casually sharing with him why we were interested and finding out why he was selling. It's amazing how much you can learn about a person in a short time if your antennas are up. We discovered that Brian was married, and, from some of the things he had mentioned, we inferred that he was having some struggles in his relationship. We learned that he lived in a home he had built just three miles down the road near the town of Sweet, but had been thinking about moving closer to the city to make things easier on his family. We felt fairly certain that he had no relationship with the Lord and wasn't particularly interested in one. He was a nice man and we liked him right off, yet we sensed that something important was missing in his life. We wondered if we would ever see Brian again.

The next day, Nancy called me at work, telling me that to her surprise Brian had called that day with a potential proposition. He had asked if he could drop by and get a quick tour of our home. We hadn't put it on the market yet but were preparing to do so, and because his advertising company was only about 15 minutes away, he came right over at her consent. Brian took a brief walk through and afterwards suggested that we might consider a straight-across trade—our home for their home with all the Timber Butte property. He said he wanted to bring his wife, Lisa, to see our place (which he did the following Saturday) and offered to show us their home that Sunday after church. In a bit of shock, Brian's wife agreed, and both visits were made. Then, on a handshake, we struck a deal. In less than one month, escrows were closed and our moving convoys passed each other on the highway that connected the two properties as we took occupancy of each other's homes.

Both properties were complicated, as many rural properties are. Things like irrigation systems, property lines and water rights caused us to stay in touch. We periodically called each other with questions, and Nancy and Lisa began to build a friendship. Lisa had been a Christian at one point in her life, but after marrying Brian (her third husband), she moved to the country and let her spiritual life slide. We discovered that Brian, who lit his next cigarette with the embers of his last, had been an alcoholic before he met Lisa and had built the house we now owned as a means of rehabilitation. His drinking had so damaged his health that he had nearly died before he met her, and he had fathered a son with a woman who lived with him during those years. It would have been easy to judge Brian. From a Christian perspective, he had plenty of flaws—and he seemed to be comfortable with most of them. Yet we liked Brian. He clearly had a wall up that caused him to be somewhat standoffish and intimidating at times. However, we believed that Brian was not only a very gifted man but also special—we just weren't sure how.

More than a year after our real estate transaction, Lisa confided in Nancy that her marriage to Brian was on the brink of divorce. Feeling that Lisa had given her permission to be honest, Nancy told Lisa that she needed to renew her faith in Christ and get back into Christian fellowship. This conversation went on for several months until finally, one Sunday morning, Lisa mustered up the nerve to announce to Brian that she was going to church. Brian said nothing, but when Lisa was about to leave, he quietly joined her. She didn't know what to say, so she didn't say anything—they just got in the car and headed toward town. That was the beginning of a great miracle that would transpire in both of their lives.

I was preaching that morning and was completely shocked when I saw Brian and Lisa walk through the door. Our church was undergoing a major expansion project at the time, and we were meeting in our gymnasium. We had added a service and packed as many chairs as we possibly could into the smaller space, but still seating was limited, to say the least. Brian and Lisa arrived slightly late that morning, and as a result the only seats left were in the front row. As always, Brian wore his hat, shorts and boots, while Lisa was classy and well dressed. They didn't go unnoticed as they were ushered past the multitudes to the very front.

The makeshift stage was small and confining, but somehow our worship leader managed to cram his entire band on it and began to lead the church in worship. The minute worship started, Brian began to weep. I'm sure he thought he was having a nervous breakdown or something, because he had always been a man in control of his emotions. He tried to hide his tears, and because everyone else in the room was engaged in worship, I'm sure that no one noticed. Afterward, I taught my message, purposefully not looking toward Brian and Lisa for fear that I might make them feel conspicuous and uncomfortable. It had taken a year and a half to get Brian to church, and I wanted it to be the best possible experience it could be for him, even in the crowded and stuffy conditions.

As the service ended, some people prayed for others while the rest of the congregation started to casually talk and visit. Nancy and I, being close by, walked up to say hello to Brian and Lisa. Brian's eyes were red, and he was wiping them with his sleeve. Realizing that it would be futile to try to conceal his emotion, he simply looked at me with an expression of bewilderment and amazement, and said in a very matter-of-fact way, "That was one hell of a band!" While many people might consider his description of worship inappropriate for church, I recognized it for what it was—a man grappling with his emotions and trying to express how his heart felt about what he had just experienced. At first, Brian didn't understand what had happened to him that morning, but later he would confess that the finger of God had pressed a seed of truth deep into his hard heart.

Brian and Lisa returned the next Sunday, wanting to know if the same thing would happen again. It did. In fact, it kept happening for months. Brian's feelings of contempt and animosity towards the Christian Church and faith began to soften and fade until he finally gave up his stubbornness and surrendered his life to God. That next spring, Nancy and I started a small group that met in our home for our new neighbors who lived in and around our small community near Timber Butte. Amazingly, Brian and Lisa drove out every week and attended. As only God could do, He brought them back to their old home to start their lives all over again. The following June, two years after our trade, I baptized Brian one stormy evening in the Payette River.

The best thing is that's not the end of the story. It was merely the beginning for Brian and Lisa. For over a year, the seed God had planted in Brian's heart remained hidden under the surface. During that time, Brian read his Bible from cover to cover, secretly investigating its truths. Nancy and I watched from a distance, not wanting to interfere in whatever God was doing, yet available if called upon.

We watched as Brian decided to quit smoking cold turkey, though we were skeptical after seeing so many others fail. No one told Brian to quit; this was something that happened during that season of invisible development when he was looking purely to God for direction and counsel. We watched as God worked on him through a season of financial difficulty, and while things began to change in his marriage and parenting. Brian became soft and compassionate, his wall of intimidation crumbling.

One day Brian announced that he wanted more; he wanted to know what the church had to offer when it came to deep discipleship. It was as if he broke out into the full light of day, hoping to absorb everything God had to offer—the truth, warmth and healing of the Son; the empowerment of the Spirit; and the deep sense of belonging and love of the Father. Not only was Brian being transformed, but God also immediately started to use him as an agent of transformation in the lives of others. He enrolled in a two-year seminary-level leadership school our church conducted and started a small group for businessmen he encountered in his professional life. At first, I was sure this was like Paul's first preaching experience in Damascus, when he got too zealous too soon, but Brian never looked back—he only pressed ahead.

Brian and Lisa eventually went on to pastor a growing country church in the same community where they once lived. They made it full circle in one sense, but have been on a straight-ahead journey in another.

Brian's story shouldn't be considered exceptional; rather, it should be the norm for Christians intent on dispensing with the perception of J.A.M.E.S. and reflecting the heart of Jesus. The Christian walk is a continual lifelong journey with lots of ebbs and flows—ups and downs. Because it advances more quickly for some than for others, it requires patience by those who are called to encourage and nurture new believers. You can't push a growing Christian to maturity any more than you can a fragile young seedling. If you try, you are in danger of up-rooting the tender sprout and stopping the growth all together. Discipleship is a delicate process that can often be discouraging. Personally I like slow growth—I trust it more. Too often, I have seen hot flashes that burn brightly but burn out quickly. I prefer long, steady, slow burns that can go the distance. Paul indicates that salvation is a long-term process when he told the Philippians to "continue to work out your salvation with fear and trembling, for it is God who works in you to will and to act according to his good purpose" (Phil. 2:12-13).

Transformation is a miracle God performs in and through us—one marked by His patience for us. We are each in an ongoing transformation process. We must change our mindset and our attitudes—two important changes that will revolutionize not only our personal worldviews but also our relationships with the world around us.

Never Underestimate Patience

When it comes to sharing our faith, patience always trumps judgment. There's something about judgment that's so final. There's no appeal—no second chance. It's simply over. Yet when we think about the people we dearly love and desire to come to the Lord, we don't give judgment a second thought. We know that God loves our friends and desires relationships with them. It may have been 20 years or more, but we're not giving up hope that God is going to transform their lives. I still have a list of friends from college whom I pray for and regularly keep in contact with—friends I deeply love and whose lives I desire to see God transform.

For every Brian in our lives, there is another name. It's the name of a person who has yet to have his or her eyes opened to the truth. But we know it's going to happen. We know we are going to have deep conversations with this person about matters of the heart—matters of faith. It's a question of *when*, not *if*.

That name in my (Jason's) dad's life was Jack. Before my father entered the ministry, he was a U.S. Air Force fighter pilot, which made for entertaining stories at the dinner table as one hand pursued the other in his dramatic retelling of aviation dogfights. It also made for interesting conversations about faith, as he shared stories about people who were so chilled to the gospel it made us shiver. Jack was one of those people.

Jack was part of my dad's squadron. None of the guys were exactly excited about having a devout Christian as part of their group. One pilot did everything he could to antagonize my father, mocking him for his zealous faith by creating a character in a comic strip that was easily identifiable as my dad. Not that my dad was a Bible thumper, but he was enthusiastic about his faith and the difference God had made in his life. He wasn't shy about sharing this fact in everyday conversation. While Jack wasn't an antagonist, he was just like everyone else in the squadron—in desperate need of God in his life.

One afternoon, Jack had a serious request of my dad: He wanted my dad to pray for his brother, who had just attempted suicide. Jack didn't reveal all the details surrounding his brother's attempt. He simply asked my dad to pray—a request my dad agreed to honor. The next day, my dad reported to Jack that he had sensed, as he was praying, that his brother was going to be fine. What Jack hadn't told my dad was that his brother had stuck a revolver in his mouth and pulled the trigger. The doctors' prognosis was that if Jack's brother survived, he would likely be in a state where he would need assistance for the rest of his life. Within two weeks, Jack's brother walked out of the hospital.

But that wasn't enough for Jack, much to my dad's dismay. It wasn't long before Jack was back to his old ways, despite the amazing miracle he had just witnessed.

Three years later, tragedy struck again in Jack's life—his wife left him. This tragedy was deeper and more personal than the previous experience with his brother. Jack needed immediate help. He wanted his wife back, so he wrote my dad a letter. My dad called him to discuss what was happening—and then Jack asked for prayer.

"I remember you praying for my brother, and God healed him," Jack said. "So I figured you could do the same and pray that my wife will come back."

"No, I'm not going to do it," my dad said.

"What?" Jack asked. "Why not?"

My dad went on to explain that God is not some genie in a magic lamp you can just rub whenever things aren't going your way. His love for us is deep and amazing, and He wants more than just our humble requests—He wants our lives. So my dad refused to pray for Jack unless he decided he wanted to get serious about following God. Once Jack decided that he did, the transformation that unfolded was remarkable, despite my dad's belief that Jack was simply agreeing so my dad would pray for him.

A few months after Jack decided to follow Christ, my parents went to visit him and his wife several states away. Jack's wife had an immediate question for my parents: "What have you done to my husband? He's never loved me like this before!" She followed that up with another surprising statement: "Whatever he's got, I want it too!" It wasn't long before their whole family began following God. After that, I never heard much about Jack until one fateful afternoon.

I walked in the door to our house after school that day and found my dad intensely watching a videotape of Jack's funeral service. It had been eight years since my dad had challenged Jack to begin following God, and their contact since that one visit had been limited to not much more than Christmas cards and family update letters in December. My dad had no idea of the depth of transformation that had occurred in Jack's life—until he watched the tape.

A steady stream of friends shared how Jack had encouraged them to follow God as a steady stream of tears flowed down my dad's face. My dad had known that Jack was following God, but he had no idea he was following God like *this*. It had taken years for Jack's heart to soften to the point where it was pliable and God could begin to work on him. My dad watched the fruit of that work right in front of his teary eyes. My dad's patience with a man who'd constructed a stone wall around his heart had paid off for the sake of the Kingdom. My dad had reflected Jesus to a man in desperate need of a Savior—and that man found and embraced his Savior long before the plane crash that killed him over Louisiana woodlands.

Don't Be in Such a Hurry

John Wesley once wrote, "Humility and patience are the surest proofs of the increase of love." We need more love to accurately reflect the heart of Jesus to those around us. Our best efforts to reflect Jesus rather than J.A.M.E.S. will fall short without an ample supply of God's love—the kind of love that transforms us from the inside first and then moves on to the outside. Without patience, we will fall back into judging others. To avoid that, it's important that we embrace God's love for us and shower it upon others, even though that's hard to do when we're ushering them toward a place they aren't ready to go just yet.

Patience is a leading hallmark of love. If we truly love those around us and want to see them come to know Jesus in a transformative way, we must be patient as God works in their hearts and continues the process of drawing others to Himself.

Chapter 3

EVERY HEAD BOWED, EVERY HEART OPENED

Arrogant → Humble

Humility, that low, sweet root, from which all heavenly virtues shoot.

Thomas Moore

When Toyota president Akio Toyoda bowed during a press conference in which the automaker was announcing its embarrassing vehicle recall, the Japanese press parsed his gesture. What exactly did his bow indicate? Contrition? Mild regret? The degree of the bow, along with its angle and context, all mattered. Some even wondered if he had tempered his bow, since a long bow interpreted as acceptance of responsibility could put Toyota at risk for future lawsuits. But the real question is this: Why did Mr. Toyoda even bow at all? Was he personally to blame for his company's faulty engineering problems? Had he worked on the assembly line that installed the poor brakes? Did he invent the car's braking system?

Why ever would he apologize for something he didn't personally do? Culturally, Mr. Toyoda's bow made sense. He needed to make an apology to save face with the company (though it couldn't be a long bow, as that might be perceived as admission of guilt and cost the company millions in lawsuits). But he also realized what it was that he represented: Toyota, the automaker giant. It wasn't about whether he was actually the one who designed or installed the brakes. The people who worked on the assembly lines will never be seen bowing on television before a press corps. They were just doing what they knew to do, more than likely unknowingly installing poor brakes. No, Toyoda's bow was about accepting responsibility for what he represented—good, bad or indifferent. The press may have assessed the level of regret by the degree and length of Mr. Toyoda's bow, but one thing is certain: Beginning his press conference with a gesture of humility was his only option.

Some people may have found Mr. Toyoda's bow quite perplexing. I (Tri) encountered such people when I introduced the idea of J.A.M.E.S. to my church, explaining that this perception of Christians is something we must deal with, regardless of whether the perception is justified. I encouraged those in our church to ask for forgiveness on behalf of the people who had hurt them whenever they met others who had been hurt by the Church. For me, this wasn't a radical idea. As a pastor, I find myself in numerous conversations with people who rage about the Church or drag behind them substantial baggage of bitterness stemming from a hurtful encounter with a Christian. Taking a defensive posture with someone who is still reeling from this kind of pain is never helpful. But there were those in our church who vehemently disagreed with me.

Instead of getting "atta boys" after my message, I was approached by a steady stream of people who were a few pitchforks and torches short of becoming a mob. "I'm not asking someone to forgive me for something I didn't do!" they would tell me. Or, "Why would I ask for forgiveness? If they're hurt, they need to tell the person who hurt them!" Based on their reactions, you would have thought I had asked them to admit to a crime. I realized this idea was tweaking people. And despite the fact that some people were leaving my church, I liked what I was seeing emerge—a deep and meaningful conversation about the art of disarming through a heart of humility.

Christians? Arrogant?

Sharing the underpinnings of your faith with someone can be tricky. If you take Jesus at His word, you have to believe that accepting His death and resurrection and then following Him is the only way to eternal life. But sharing this tenet of our faith often sends people running from the room while showering us with accusations of being "arrogant" and "closed-minded." Why? Is it really arrogant to share what you believe, even if it means acknowledging that what you believe allows no leeway for other religions' ideas about getting to heaven?

No one with any integrity can say that Christianity in and of itself—devoid of all the religious trappings that Jesus railed against—is arrogant. In fact, it's just the opposite. Jesus was the humble King, willing to die for something He didn't do. He called His followers to likewise walk in humility, rejecting the way of the world for a life that was grounded in God's Word. This is the upside-down nature of God's kingdom. In a world of self-promotion and "me first," Jesus calls us to promote others and be last for the sake of His kingdom.

What people *do* (sometimes rightfully so) find arrogant is the *way* Christians present the gospel. A "my way or the highway" approach to evangelism pales in comparison to a gentle invitation to "the way of Jesus." It's simply antagonistic. Jesus never twisted any arms to get people to believe; He simply issued an invitation that came accompanied by a life that embodied the truths He taught. Instead of raging against the pagan culture of His day (something Christians are great at doing in the twenty-first century), Jesus' outbursts of anger were directed toward the religious leaders whose legalism and hypocrisy kept followers mired in mediocrity instead of experiencing the fullness of a relationship with God. Jesus knew that the unreligious people were blinded by the world. They couldn't see the truth. So, He took compassion on them. He healed them. He shared with them who He was. He loved them, no matter what dejected state they were in. All of this was done with striking humility—an example of love and grace that gives us a blueprint for sharing with those who are seeking and have open hearts. Non-believers often claim that any presentation of the gospel due to its very nature ("Jesus is the only way") is arrogant. That is an unfair characterization, yet we must be careful to ensure that the tone and manner in which we present the gospel doesn't have a hint of arrogance to it. Nonetheless, humility sometimes seems like a forgotten element today when it comes to sharing our faith with those who desperately need to hear the good news.

Feeling pushed into a corner by our culture, many Christians in the U.S. figure the only way to respond is to push back. Many evangelical leaders encourage us to "take back our Christian nation." If you had spent the last 50 years on another planet and just returned to earth, you would think there is an actual physical assault being waged against Christians by unbelievers. The fact is, opposition to the Christian message is nothing new. It has been going on for almost 2,000 years now. The heart of Christ flies in the face of a debased culture—a culture that is not swayed by strong-arm tactics but instead is won over through love. Instead of pushing back, we should be offering hugs—embracing those whose real beef isn't with God but with J.A.M.E.S. Christians. These hurt and wary people need us to present God's good news with all humility.

Consider the apostle Paul's charge to the church in Ephesus: "Be completely humble and gentle; be patient, bearing with one another in love" (Eph. 4:2). *Completely humble.* This stands in stark contrast to arrogance. When we receive an invitation to speak from those who have yet to have a life-changing encounter with Jesus, ramming the truth down their throats prevents them from having the opportunity to savor redemption's elixir. Like a fine wine, it must be swirled around to be recognized for what it truly is—amazing grace. When some people realize this, they are ready to take large gulps from the cup. But others are less willing. They need more convincing—and more time to ponder the ramifications of what following Christ will mean for their lives. When we are sharing God's love and grace with others, it can only be done with complete humility.

We must resist the urge to become indignant with the skeptics and instead let ourselves be filled with grace. The Bible contains many accounts of people who "tested" God, either questioning His methods or doubting His resolve. Job, Gideon, Elijah, Jonah—these men all wrestled with the way God was doing things in their lives. Yet God showed grace to them as He taught them valuable lessons in trusting Him. Then there's Thomas—doubting Thomas—the disciple who just couldn't believe it was Jesus standing in front of him. Never mind that he had spent years following Jesus around. That made no difference to him. Thomas wanted to put his fingers in those nail-pierced hands and know that it was Jesus. Here is how Jesus responded to His skepticism:

> A week later his disciples were in the house again, and
> Thomas was with them. Though the doors were locked,

Jesus came and stood among them and said, "Peace be with you!" Then he said to Thomas, "Put your finger here; see my hands. Reach out your hand and put it into my side. Stop doubting and believe."

Thomas said to him, "My Lord and my God!"

Then Jesus told him, "Because you have seen me, you have believed; blessed are those who have not seen and yet have believed" (John 20:26-29).

In our zealous state, we want to *make* everyone believe. We aren't patient enough to let their Thomas experiences play out. *Believe and believe now*, we plead. *Time is of the essence.* And it is, but maybe not in the way that we think it is. We push people with phrases such as "you never know when your number is up" or "you never know when your time on earth will be finished." Then there are even more direct approaches: "What if you get into a car wreck and die on the way home tonight?"

While there is an urgency to begin walking with Jesus (and what we are saying is true because anyone *could* die in a wreck on their way home at any time), we are trying to evoke an emotional response from someone—a response driven by fear rather than marked by faith. Such a strategy is not based in the patient humility that God has. He waits a long time for many of us to begin our relationships with Him. While technically one day could make all the difference, that fact shouldn't be something we push on people just to get them to begin their relationships with Christ. We should allow them to work through their doubts in God's timing, because then when they finally do arrive at the place where they decide they want to follow God, it will be much richer than if it had been a pressure-packed moment, induced by guilt or fear.

The theologian N. T. Wright makes some great observa-
tions about Thomas:

> Thomas, bless him, acts as we would expect. (It is in
> this gospel that the rather flat characters in the other
> accounts come up in more three-dimensional reality.)
> The dour, dogged disciple who suggested they might
> as well go with Jesus, if only to die with him (11.16),
> who complained that Jesus hadn't made things any-
> thing like clear enough (14.5), just happened to be the
> one who was somewhere else on the first Easter day.
> He sees the others excited, elated, unable to contain
> their joy. He's not going to be taken in.
>
> Fair enough. At the end, Jesus issues a gentle re-
> buke to Thomas for needing to see before he would be-
> lieve; but we notice that the beloved disciple describes
> his own arrival at faith in the same way. "He saw, and
> believed" (verse 8). This isn't, then, so much a rebuke to
> Thomas; it's more an encouragement to those who
> come later, to people of subsequent generations. We
> are all "blessed" when, without having seen the risen
> Lord for ourselves, we nevertheless believe in him.[1]

Thomas regularly gets blasted and is branded as the
doubting disciple. But he represents most of us. None of us
will physically stick our fingers in Jesus' nail-pierced hands in
this lifetime, but we still want to see God for ourselves. We
want to experience the power of God in our lives. We want to
realize the fullness of God's grace. Once we do, we want nothing else. Yet for some reason, we try to rush other people
through this process in the name of evangelism, forgetting
that we discovered Christ at our own slow pace.

Once we begin following Jesus, we don't just blindly muddle our way through the Christian life. If we're serious about our faith, we look at what we're doing and hold it up to the light of who Jesus is. We should never just assume that we're "doing fine" and are well on our way to becoming "super Christians." The reality is that we need to know how we're doing, and there is only one viable litmus test in the Christian walk: Jesus Himself.

Jonathan Edwards described our need to see where we stand with God—to evaluate how we are progressing in our journey with Him:

The surest way to know our gold, is to look upon it and examine it in God's furnace, where he tries it for that end, that we may see what it is. If we have a mind to know whether a building stands strong or no, we must look upon it when the wind blows. . . . If we would know whether a staff be strong, or a rotten broken reed, we must observe it when it is leaned on, and weight is borne upon it. If we would weigh ourselves justly, we must weigh ourselves in God's scales that he makes use of to weigh us.[2]

When we examine ourselves in light of who Jesus is, we see where we are. We see how far we have to go. We see just how brightly—or how dimly—we reflect Jesus. Such self-assessment is a wise course of action.

Just as people who have embraced God wrestled with Him, so too do those who have yet to accept Him into their lives. We must make room for God to work in their lives, presenting the gospel with humility—not pressure—so that they may see God's heart for themselves and experience His powerful love and redeeming grace.

Understanding Authentic Humility

A number of years ago, I (Tri) felt a deep conviction to preach a series of messages on Christianity and the environment. Since no pastor I knew in the evangelical community had even broached the subject, it felt like a pioneer venture. I was not entirely sure what to expect, so I was pleasantly surprised when my message hit a major nerve not only in our church, but also all across the country. I recognized that God was blessing my efforts, and feeling inspired to keep going, I called Jason and told him we needed to write a book that challenged the greater Church to do what we were doing. The book was titled *Saving God's Green Earth: Rediscovering the Church's Responsibility to Environmental Stewardship*, and it has been used in a powerful way to bring awareness to the Church about our need to embrace the responsibility of creation care.

The uproar our initiative caused was soon heard beyond the Church. PBS came to Boise to shoot a Bill Moyer documentary titled *Is God Green?* that helped bring even more attention to the subject. Shortly after the documentary aired, I received a call from a man named Joe. Joe was extremely pleasant and very affirming of all we were doing at the Boise Vineyard. He was a leader in one of the most influential and powerful environmental lobbying agencies in our state. I had heard of Joe's organization and knew it was an extremely liberal group politically, not unlike the Sierra Club or Greenpeace. In my previous evangelical life, I would have considered this group the "enemy"—and vice versa. We were clearly on opposite sides of the red-and-blue table. That's why I was shocked when Joe asked me to be the keynote speaker at his organization's annual meeting that year. I frankly couldn't believe it and considered the invitation nothing short of a miracle. With fear and trepidation, I accepted.

The meeting was to be held at a classic historical lodge in the Sawtooth Mountains, three hours northeast of Boise. I knew the place well, because it was the very place Nancy and I had stayed while on our honeymoon 35 years before. A week before the conference, Joe contacted my office again. There was a clear tone of nervousness in his voice. He informed me that when word got out that an evangelical pastor was slated to speak at their annual conference, a number of their members pushed back. They couldn't believe Joe would invite (in many of their minds) a judgmental, self-righteous evangelical pastor to talk about the environment. Immediately, I assumed Joe was going to withdraw the invitation; instead, he simply requested that I refrain from praying. He felt that prayer would be over the top and more than his constituents could handle. I agreed but knew I would be frantically crying out to God for help—just not out loud.

The day of the conference finally arrived, and Nancy and I drove up and checked into our room on the shoreline of Red Fish Lake. The towering peaks of the Sawtooth range rose some 12,000 feet above us. The setting was so magnificent it reminded me of the miracle of creation and the reason God had me there. Unfortunately, the confidence that view inspired didn't last long. We didn't know a soul, and every insecurity rose up in me. This was clearly not my tribe—I didn't know a soul—and those old wounded feelings and insecurities rooted clear back in my junior high days tried to manifest.

That night I couldn't sleep. I was the first speaker on the docket the next morning, and for the life of me, I couldn't think of what I should say or even how I would start. The words of Jesus came to mind: "Whenever you are arrested and brought to trial, do not worry beforehand about what to say. Just say whatever is given you at the time, for it is not you speaking, but the Holy Spirit" (Mark 13:11). Though I wasn't (technically) on trial, those were comforting words for my restless heart. Still, I was far from full of faith right then and didn't have the confidence to believe God would back my act. For all the speaking experience I had, I was shaken and scared. Never before had I spoken in a place where I would be so scrutinized.

It took awhile, but morning finally came. Nancy and I got ready and headed for the dining hall. People were extremely friendly and cordial—but I soon realized that they didn't know who I was. After breakfast, everyone gathered in the main hall, and Joe welcomed us to the annual gathering. He conducted some business, shared some housekeeping items, and then began his speaker introduction. Joe shared about the Moyer documentary on PBS and about my book. I could feel the tension in the room. The moment had come, and I still didn't know what I would say or how I would begin.

When I stood up and made my way forward, I saw that a number of people who had met Nancy and me earlier that morning appeared surprised. I think our normality didn't match their image of an evangelical leader. I took the microphone from Joe, thanked him for such a cordial introduction, and opened my mouth to begin. That's when God showed up and fulfilled His promise: "Just say whatever is given you at the time, for it is not you speaking, but the Holy Spirit."

My first words were words of sincere apology. I asked for forgiveness from those in attendance. I started by saying, "On behalf of many evangelicals—not all, but many—I want to ask your forgiveness for how poorly we have done concerning the very thing you folks have been so passionate about. We have been negligent, and we have been wrong." I didn't just *say* I was sorry. I really felt it, and the emotion God put in me at that moment changed the climate of the room.

I went on to admit that Christians had been disobedient to God's commission to care for His creation. Then I spent the next 30 minutes giving them a Bible study in both the Old and New Testaments, demonstrating that God had charged His people with being good stewards of the earth. Not only was the audience cordial and polite the whole time I was speaking, but they also seemed sincerely interested in what I was saying. It was one of the richest and most memorable speaking engagements I've ever experienced. From the moment I asked their forgiveness, I could tell that I not only had their ears but had also won their hearts. Nancy and I made some wonderful friends that day—an opportunity we likely would have missed had I not said, in a manner of speaking, "Please forgive J.A.M.E.S."

Several weeks later, an article appeared on the front page of *The Idaho Statesman* reporting on the event. People were quoted as saying that they appreciated my talk because it made them rethink their perspectives on faith. Nancy and I joined Joe's organization that day, and God gave us relationships with people we most likely would never have had the privilege of knowing under the circumstances of our normal Christian life. That was a big lesson for me. I learned the power of authentic humility, not to gain access into the lives of non-churched people, but to fall genuinely in love with them.

So often our approach to evangelism comes from a place of arrogance—an assumption that we have all the answers and others don't. We treat other people as if they are stupid, when in fact they are merely blind. We would never assume that a physically blind person is unintelligent just because he or she can't see. We might hold the secrets to eternal life with God, but that does not somehow make us superior to those who have yet to accept Christ and begin their journey with Him.

Francis Frangipane explains humility this way:

> I have learned that much of my spiritual progress does
> not come directly from God, but through my ability
> to humble myself and hear Him speak through imper-
> fect people. In fact, I have discovered that it pleases
> Him to hide His manifold wisdom in a variety of peo-
> ple and denominational perspectives. I know that the
> more I humble myself to others, the broader my un-
> derstanding of God has actually become.[3]

Only when we realize that we don't know it all can we begin to learn more. We also must realize that in our efforts to
share the love of Christ with others, we can learn from them as
we act in humility. God will use any situation—or any person—
to teach us if we have the right hearts.

Opening Hearts

Before I (Tri) entered into the ministry, I served as a school
teacher. Oftentimes, students asked me questions that I just
could not answer. Instead of trying to fudge my way through
and create a false sense of intellect, I would turn around and
ask the students what they thought. Sometimes the questions
developed into class projects that involved everyone. Many of
these projects turned out to be landmark moments in the
learning experience of these students, who remembered so
much more vividly the answer they eventually discovered than
they would have any explanation I could have given them.

Likewise in my experience as a Christian, I have found
that entering a room full of skeptics with a bowed head will
open hearts. Presenting yourself as the all-knowing oracle

only dilutes the message you are bringing. People are put off when you fire off canned answers to their serious questions. A perception of arrogance is the defeating byproduct.

One of the most effective teaching tools any educator can use is that of getting students to discover answers for themselves. For example, it's one thing to be told that smoking is bad for you; it's another thing to see the actual tar built up in the lung of a deceased smoker. Taking this approach to talking with people about issues of faith is immensely more successful than peppering them with a list of facts. Not surprisingly, self-discovery is exactly the approach Jesus used when presenting truths and admonishing people to live more godly lives.

In Luke 10:25-37, we read the well-known story of the Good Samaritan. As with most of Jesus' teachings, there are many rich layers to what He was communicating to His disciples through this parable. Throughout the Gospels, the theme of Jesus' dissatisfaction with the prevailing religious leaders of the day often recurs. He frequently exposed their fraudulent, hypocritical lifestyles. However, when it came time to get people to move from one way of thinking to another, Jesus wanted His followers to have their own "Ah-ha!" moments.

As Jesus began telling the parable of the Good Samaritan, two ideologies seemed to clash with each other—the first being that we should help those in need, and the second being that ritual and "being clean" in the house of God superseded any immediate needs, no matter how urgent those needs were. This was Jesus' way of demonstrating that being religious didn't always equate to being godly. Jesus made this point over and over in His ministry—and He did it with the utmost humility. Surely it would have been much easier for Jesus to walk into the synagogues with His verbal arguments ready to be released on some unsuspecting Pharisee. But Jesus also wanted to demonstrate that a convincing argument rarely results in a changed heart. Hearts aren't transformed through well-rehearsed speeches; they're transformed when they see the truth and power of God demonstrated through a humble man or woman of God.

> "Which of these three do you think was a neighbor to the man who fell into the hands of robbers?" The expert in the law replied, "The one who had mercy on him." Jesus told him, "Go and do likewise" (Luke 10:36-37).

Even the expert, whose initial purpose had simply been to try to trip Jesus up, figured out what the right answer was before Jesus issued the next action step. How open would his heart have been if Jesus had unleashed a furious rant against religious leaders? How effective would His message have been? If our hearts remain humble, we have a much greater chance of impacting people with the truth of the gospel. When we follow Jesus' example, we embody grace and truth in action and more clearly reflect Him to those around us.

Meet People Where They Are

One of the most detrimental effects programmatic evangelism has had on many believers involves the expectations they have after they present the gospel to someone. If a person hearing the message doesn't opt for the next-step prayer, the person sharing the message considers it a failed attempt at evangelism. Christians console themselves with phrases like "I planted some seeds today" or "all in God's time." But deep down, it feels like failure, especially when Mr. Evangelism Guy is going to report at Bible study that he prayed the sinner's prayer with three people this week—and it's only Wednesday.

As a pastor, I often feel like the deck is stacked against me when it comes to sharing about my faith, despite the fact that I have a platform to teach from each Sunday. Outside of church, I get stonewalled by people's best defensive postures the second I mention that I am a pastor. I sometimes wonder what it would be like if I just told people I randomly meet that I manage a small ranch (which I do). The resistance would probably be much less. However, I always want to be ready to share the heart of Christ with others—in deed or in words, whichever is most appropriate.

When you live in an isolated area, as Nancy and I do, neighbors can be your lifeline. Getting to know them is of utmost importance. Over the years, we have taken full advantage of this ranch culture to build some great relationships with people from all walks of life. We have hosted "block party" barbecues and invited neighbors over for dinner. On these occasions, my neighbor card trumps my pastor card—and people share their life stories with us.

Two of the neighbors we have developed great relationships with over the years are Greg and his wife. Greg has faced more challenges and disappointments than most people I know, yet he still maintains a positive outlook on life and is ready to help a neighbor in need at a moment's notice. We have had talks about his hang-ups with the Church and God—but I have neither rejected him for his skepticism nor loaded my theological guns to shoot holes in his thinking. As a result, he has opened up to me more.

Recently, Greg blessed us in an unexpected way. He came to me and said that he wanted to give us one of the cows he was raising. As our church thrives on being outside of our building's walls during the week, we have developed a reputation in our community—the kind of reputation that would make any pastor proud. We are known for how we love those in the community. Granted, our outreach is not always perfect, but it is abundant. Through the years, Greg has heard those stories multiple times and wanted to do something to give back. So he gave one of the most extravagant gifts he could give: a grass-fed steer. When I asked him why, he said he simply wanted to bless the volunteers in our church with a steak dinner for all they do in our community.

When I first wrote about Greg, before this book reached any editors, I concluded with this statement: "Greg's story is far from over, but I know God is at work in his life." However, it wasn't that far. Before this book was finished, Greg realized that his body wasn't going to be able to fight off the ill effects of diabetes forever. He called me one evening and asked me to pray with him to receive Christ. He didn't know how much time he had left, but he had decided that however much it was, he wanted to spend it as a follower of Jesus. Plenty of people had talked about Jesus, God and Christianity to Greg—but he told me that he was drawn to the authenticity Nancy and I had shown him in speaking about our faith. (I'm not one to sugar-coat anything, particularly the gospel.) Though Greg had long been a skeptic, his cynical heart could not continue to put up a barrier to Christlike love. Greg passed away a week later.

I had the privilege of officiating his funeral—an eclectic gathering of people who knew and loved Greg. Because of his kind heart, Greg had touched many people in our small mountain community. There were his friends who were draining a keg at the funeral. There were also his friends who were elders in the local Mormon ward. Greg may not have had the chance to tell everyone about the amazing thing God had done in his life, but I did that day.

When I approach relationships with the heart of Christ—one that genuinely wants to get to know people for who they are—I find it easier to love them. If I were to labor under the burden of trying to get someone to say a prayer, I would feel more like a salesperson than an ambassador of Christ. Even with the most honest of salespeople, you're still always aware that they are selling you something. I don't want to sell anything. I simply want my life to speak for itself. When I begin talking about my faith, I want it to be because I have been given not only permission but also an invitation to talk to someone about it.

Adios, Arrogance

If we desire to see humility rather than arrogance emerge from our hearts, we must think back to the time when we first began following Christ. What was it that drew us to God? Was it some convincing argument from a friend or pastor? Or was it our experiencing a brokenness that we knew only God—a gentle God—could heal? What won you over? What always wins you over? Do you root for the brash athlete who thinks he or she is the world's greatest? Or do you root for the soft-spoken athlete who works hard and accepts praise and acclaim with sincere humility?

When people are wrong, they are almost always reluctant to admit it. Intrinsically, people try to save face. So, is a hard-hitting approach to sharing the gospel with people—one that says, "I'm right and you're wrong . . . and you're going to burn in hell if you don't agree with me"—the best strategy? Or would presenting the gospel by living it out daily be a better way? Which method gives people space to save face?

I'm sure there will be some people who are thinking right now, *How will people know they're going to hell if we don't tell them?*

Don't mistake a humble approach to sharing the gospel for a watered-down gospel. The truth still needs to be spoken; however, the way we deliver the truth and the timing with which we do it are almost as important as the truthful words themselves.

As the apostle Paul sought to help the leaders in Ephesus understand how to handle the people in their church who were being swayed by every teaching, he gave them—and us—some powerful advice:

> Speaking the truth in love, we will in all things grow up into him who is the Head, that is, Christ. From him the whole body, joined and held together by every supporting ligament, grows and builds itself up in love, as each part does its work (Eph. 4:15-16).

Speaking the truth in love—that's an idea easier to pontificate about than walk out. But it's necessary whenever we are presenting the truth, whether it be to new believers still not firmly grounded in their faith or to skeptics desperately seeking answers about God. As we grasp this balance, we will continue to look more and more like Christ. In the process, humility will become a trademark of our lives and our relationships with others—and the "arrogant Christian" label won't be applied any longer.

But this book is about more than simply erasing labels—it's about understanding that if we're going to call ourselves followers of Jesus, we must be committed to reflecting Him to the world. There's a significant difference between trying to get people to come to church and making disciples. While countless conferences in our country each year focus on "how to grow your church," that "growth" centers on the number of people attending Sunday services. Instead, we need to be

Chapter 4

HOW KIND ARE YOU?

Mean-spirited → Kind

You can safely assume you've created God in your own image when it turns out that God hates all the same people you do.
Anne Lamott

When you strive to be righteous, a dangerous thing can happen—you can start to *think* you're more righteous than you really are. It's at that moment that you're likely to don a black robe and begin banging a gavel on everyone else's unrighteousness. Instead of being a grace-filled Christian, you transform into an angry, self-righteous person. In short, you become a Pharisee.

I (Jason) used to bristle whenever I heard unbelievers say they thought Christians were mean. For some reason, my defensive instincts kicked in. I used to think that attacks on Christians were equal to attacks on Jesus Himself. I still have to suppress that natural inclination when I hear an accusation of meanness levied against fellow Christians. But the reality is that it's true . . . sometimes. There are a lot of mean people in the world—and while many of them do not profess to be Christians, some of them do.

While living in the Deep South, where almost everyone claims to be a Christian, I worked at a newspaper—which generally means enduring endless mocking of Christians by other newsroom employees. The profession seems to attract as many unbelievers as possible. Cynicism runs rampant through a newsroom, because each person is dealing with entities and people who are corrupt. It's a never-ending task of alerting the local community to the duplicity of the area's leaders. It's almost impossible not to become cynical.

Reporters question everything and always surmise that there is a strong money trail odor wafting through the office of every political office holder. If it's hypocritical and unbecoming, it gets printed. Outrageous stories about inane things Christians were doing in the name of God seemed to come across the national newswire with regularity. Inevitably, those stories would garner ridicule (though I must admit that most news people are equal opportunity mockers). I didn't mind that too much because, while I take my faith seriously, I've learned you can't take people and their well-intentioned but misguided blanket statements too seriously. Besides, there is humor to be found in the Christian culture—acknowledging that doesn't mean being a heretic.

What I didn't find humorous were the regular failings of the handful of other outspoken Christians in the newsroom. Non-Christian employees noticed these missteps as well, and often commented on them: *Can you believe she said that? I thought she was a Christian!* or *I would never go to a church that teaches people to act like that!* Frankly, I can see how confusing it must be to people who haven't yet chosen to follow Jesus. Until you begin a journey with Christ, you expect everyone who professes to be a Christian to fully reflect Jesus. That's the goal, but once you begin your own journey, you realize that you—and everyone else—fall woefully short. I felt like I had to keep covering—and apologizing—for my fellow Christians' actions when such derisive comments were slung in my direction.

Then one day *it* happened. By *it*, I mean the most memorable event that happened to me within a newsroom during my journalism career. I played a prank on a Christian coworker. I thought it was harmless and that she would think it was funny too. I was wrong. She was deeply offended by what I did and even went so far as to threaten to sue the newspaper over my actions. In a word, it was ugly. And I was wrong.

However, this was my big chance—my opportunity to demonstrate what a follower of Jesus would do. So, I humbled myself and asked her to forgive me. I did it privately, and again publicly. I wanted my fellow employees—many of whom thought I shouldn't apologize—to realize that Christians could resolve conflict even in such tense circumstances. We were going to work it out and be a light in a dark place. Unfortunately, the situation blew up in my face. The woman refused to talk to me for weeks. I was distraught and didn't know what else I could do. I thought it would blow over after a while, but it didn't. She made such a fuss that my superiors made a conciliatory gesture in her favor and suspended me from work for two days.

What's funny (in a sad way) is that this woman had always been nice to me. Before, she saw us as members of the same team—two Christians, a brother and a sister, in a newsroom full of people bent on antagonizing us. But the moment any conflict arose, I was as good as dead to her. I never had another positive interaction with her after that. Even worse, she was the loudest and proudest Christian in the newsroom. Following our incident, more comments than ever flowed from her about how "Christian" she was.

Tri Robinson & Jason Chatraw • www.regalbooks.com

While our church was discussing what it meant to reflect the heart of Jesus, we created a blog that stirred up some interesting conversations and resulted in some great insights by people in our congregation who had been thinking about these concepts. One of the most gripping comments came from a lady named Camille, who spoke to the problem of how Christians are perceived:

> I think one of the first things we have got to own as Christians is that as long as we are perceived in a certain light, it is a reality. What I mean is that we can debate how we're seen and who is responsible for misconceptions—we can share anecdotes and our own experiences. But that won't get us anywhere until we just admit that as long as SOMEONE thinks poorly of Christians (and therefore Christianity, Jesus and God), we have work to do.

We might all cringe when we see another news story about a Christian doing something ridiculous in Jesus' name, but there's really only one thing we can do about it: pursue the heart of God for our lives so we can more clearly reflect Jesus to the world around us. When it comes to the perception of how unkind Christians are, we do have a lot of work to do.

Come As You Are,
You *Might* Be Loved

In the late 1980s, the Lord started to stir Nancy's and my (Tri's) hearts to plant a new church in Boise, Idaho. For a number of reasons, Nancy had more faith for such a venture than I did. She not only had a deep and abiding trust in God, but she also had much more confidence in my abilities than I did. The thought of moving 800 miles from Southern California, and everything I was familiar with, to a place where I had zero relationships to establish and pastor my first church scared me to death. I had to know for certain that God was into it and would back my act.

During our time of decision making, we found ourselves in the heart of the remote Idaho wilderness, camped next to the Middle Fork of the Salmon River—ironically also known as the River of No Return. It was a time of spiritual agitation for me as I wrestled with my uncertainty and lack of confidence while asking God for a clear word—not only for guidance about whether we were to plant the new church, but also for vision concerning what kind of a church He wanted. On that trip, God did what only He could do. He spoke to me in a very non-conventional way, setting me on a course of resolve to do what I otherwise would have believed to be impossible. I had climbed a mountain that towered above our river camp to pray concerning this matter of hearing from God. While there, I miraculously found a yellow balloon that contained a message. I wouldn't make such a big deal out of this if it hadn't been for the fact that at that very time I was asking God for a specific word—preferably something scriptural. I needed to know what kind of church I was to build if I was to build one at all.

Here's the message I found in the balloon (at the top of a mountain in the heart of the biggest wilderness area in the continental United States): "First John 4:7: 'Children let us love one another.'" The balloon had been released months or maybe even years earlier by a small boy named Michael in a Sunday School class in Eastern Idaho. As I sat on that mountainside, meditating in amazement on what I had found, I clearly heard the Lord say, "I don't care where you do it, but I want you to go build a church that loves people." Then I felt certain I heard God ask me if I wanted to build that church in Boise, Idaho. With tears filling my eyes, I replied with determination and even passion, "Yes I do!" One year later, we found ourselves in Idaho, along with 12 other committed families, starting a small church plant that would become the Vineyard of Boise.

The church grew rapidly over the next few years—possibly, in some ways, too rapidly for the sake of our young fellowship's own culture and health. From the beginning, we raised the spiritual banner, "Go Love People!" over everything we did. In those early days, we decided to substitute small round bistro tables scattered throughout our auditorium for more traditional theater-style seating. We adopted this concept from the mother church we had come from in Southern California.

Our former pastor, Brent Rue, was a product of the Jesus Movement and believed tables were a statement of relationship above religion. We inherited this ideology, believing as Brent did that most people desire intimacy and authentic relationship—longings that would be reflected in this style of seating. It had become a major distinctive in the Southern California church, as it soon did in the Boise church. People started to refer to us as the church that sat around tables. Our style of worship was soon perceived as being unconventional as well, and while that repelled some who saw us as too nonconforming and even strange, the nontraditional worship drew others to us. We constantly communicated to all who came that our worship style was simply another statement of desiring relationship and loving people.

Right from the beginning, we built ministry that served our community in loving ways and tried to stay obedient to the call to love not just the downtrodden and the poor, but all whom God put in our path. Early on we printed bumper stickers that read, "Come as you are, You'll be loved." We advertised ourselves as an agency destined to love people—no matter who they were, where they came from, or even what they had done in the past—no matter what. Our intent was to accept, include and love everyone God gave us. The credo to "Go love people" served our young church well—at least for a while.

Cultural changes don't happen overnight, but sometimes it feels that way. I remember one Sunday morning observing something in my congregation that deeply disturbed me. From the beginning, the vision for sitting around tables had included the idea of inviting new unchurched visitors to join with our committed members at the tables, even sharing food together. It had been our practice to serve muffins and coffee at our services, noting that friends always shared food together. We did this for the purpose of being deliberate concerning building new relationships. This one particular morning, I noticed one of our regularly attending families hoarding their table even to the point of shooing away a new family, saying out loud so everyone could hear, "This is our table. We sit here every Sunday morning during this service. You need to move!"

I was devastated—and although I didn't correct the people in error on the spot, I did consider it, and I even thought about doing it in a way that wasn't likely to be very loving. But anger isn't always the best means for real change, and I knew I had to do something everyone would remember. So I pondered what I had observed and prayed about how to confront what I was noticing as a change in our culture. I knew a credo statement was only words once it drifted from the DNA of the church culture, and I felt that one of the primary roles of a senior pastor was to be a cultural engineer. How could I get my point across in a way that would bring about lasting change?

I let nearly a month go by before I pulled the trigger on the plan I concocted in an attempt to bring us back to our original culture of love. We had used up the supply of "Come as you are, You'll be loved" bumper stickers and were about to print a new batch. I made the decision to drop the second half of the phrase—"You'll be loved"—from the new printing. I had hundreds of the bumper stickers made in preparation for the coming Sunday morning's message. In addition to the new stickers, I also designed several slides portraying other slogans I had been considering. Our new stickers could say, "Come as you are—You *might* be loved" or maybe, "Come as you are, you might be loved but there's no guarantee!"

I made several variations, all communicating in humorous but serious ways that we had lost something very precious and rich in our culture. I knew by their reactions that people heard me that morning. Though there was a lot of laughter, it was clearly nervous laughter, and it seemed obvious that nearly everyone got the message. Then I handed out the new bumper stickers that omitted the second half of the credo statement. I told the congregation that if after a year we had demonstrated a changed heart, we would go back to the original statement.

Our desire was to make authentic Christian disciples who truly shared and reflected the loving heart of God in our every-day lives. To post a bumper sticker stating that we were a people of love and then, for example, cut someone off in traffic or swear at another driver for cutting us off was not authentic but hypocritical. Everyone knew that we didn't want to become J.A.M.E.S. Christians in our community; rather, we wanted to provide a true and authentic reflection of Jesus. That was our goal and our passion. As the pastor of a growing church, I soon realized how quickly the DNA of a well-meaning group of people could mutate from the purity they set out to pursue if their leadership didn't keep watch over things like behavioral patterns. I had to be willing to confront negative issues, make strategic adjustments, and bring change as needed.

Now, after some 24 years of development, I can honestly say with confidence that the Vineyard of Boise has made great strides toward becoming the Christian agency it intended to be from the very beginning—an agency of God's love.

Why Christians Can Be Unkind

As a pastor's kid, I (Jason) learned firsthand just how unkind Christians can be. Since I was around my dad all the time, I knew he wasn't perfect. He once preached a sermon about how we need to bless those who curse us, and his real-life example included bad drivers who cut us off in traffic. I gently reminded him of his sermon a few days later, when a woman peeled out in front of us at an intersection—and he wasn't exactly blessing her. He immediately apologized to us, and the following Sunday, he even confessed to the congregation his failure to live up to his own preaching. But I knew my dad's heart. He was intent on serving and following God. If there's a more godly man on the planet, I would like to meet him.

That's why it was difficult for me to listen to my dad share painful stories of how certain church members treated him. Like most longtime pastors, my dad is fairly thick-skinned. Of course, he doesn't like hearing people say negative things about him, but he's long past the stage of finding his worth in how many compliments he receives about his sermons on Sundays (even though I find most of them profound and encouraging). But there were times when the attacks were intensely personal. Some leaders didn't just dislike my dad's preaching; they disliked *him*. Some people went to great lengths to undermine his leadership, distorting the truth and riling up other members just to cast my dad in a poor light. They hurled nasty accusations at him and levied false charges. Then I had to watch him cry. This incredible man who wanted nothing more than to serve God was reduced to choking back tears about painful experiences with people in his church. Even cuddly sheep bite.

People's perceptions of Christians as extraordinarily mean stem from the fact that virtually everyone has high standards for those who consider themselves followers of Jesus. Even most non-believers would agree that Jesus wasn't a mean person. So it makes sense to think that His followers would reflect the kindness He demonstrated while on earth.

Quantifying whether Christians are meaner than non-believers is a difficult task. But the truth is, people shouldn't have any reason to think Christians are unkind at all. We should be the kindest and gentlest people on the planet—people who exude the love of God in everything we do. Unfortunately, as mentioned in the previous chapter, we aren't whole people yet. We make mistakes and mishandle relationships. We blow up and get mad. We can even be cruel. We can embody J.A.M.E.S. and not even realize it.

Instead of walking in grace toward others and reflecting the true heart of Christ, we tend to get swept up in the current of criticism running through our culture. We look at others and pick their flaws apart. We expect everyone to be kind to us—and when they aren't, we get upset and revert to our fleshly instincts. Prove that we're right and they're wrong. Justify our actions and diminish theirs. Don't get mad—get even.

When it comes to our own mistakes, we count on grace to cover our imperfection. But other people? There's no margin for error in their lives. They should be made to suffer for what they have done to us. In essence, we've chosen to put aside Jesus' teaching about forgiveness in favor of assuaging the pain we feel. We act just like non-believers. How can we reflect Jesus when we act no differently than everyone else around us? How are others supposed to see the difference God makes in our lives when we choose to blatantly ignore Jesus' words?

William Shakespeare got it:

The quality of mercy is not strain'd,
It droppeth as the gentle rain from heaven
Upon the place beneath. It is twice blessed:
It blesseth him that gives and him that takes.[1]

Now consider these words about kindness from Romans 2:

Therefore you have no excuse, O man, every one of you who judges. For in passing judgment on another you condemn yourself, because you, the judge, practice the very same things. We know that the judgment of God rightly falls on those who practice such things. Do you suppose, O man— you who judge those who practice such things and yet do them yourself—that you will escape the judgment of God? Or do you presume on the riches of his kindness and forbearance and patience, not knowing that God's kindness is meant to lead you to repentance? (Rom. 2:1-4, *ESV*).

God's kindness is meant to lead us to repentance. It's that important. When we're kind, we're reflecting the ingredient that draws us to God.

Examine Your Kindness

Given the importance of kindness in reflecting God's desire to draw people to Himself, it is essential that we take time to examine where we are with kindness in our own lives. The real testing moment comes when we take time to examine where we are with kindness in our own lives. Are we kind only to those who are kind to us? Or are we kind to everyone, regardless of how they treat us?

It is easy to be nice to people when they are nice to us. Who doesn't respond well to a pleasant hello or a smile from a friend, family member or co-worker? When someone is courteous, interacting kindly with that person comes fairly naturally. But Jesus wasn't giving out gold stars for such behavior.

> If you love those who love you, what benefit is that to you? For even sinners love those who love them. And if you do good to those who do good to you, what benefit is that to you? For even sinners do the same. And if you lend to those from whom you expect to receive, what credit is that to you? Even sinners lend to sinners, to get back the same amount (Luke 6:32-34, *ESV*).

In God's kingdom, the most trying moments are the ones that prove our faith. Jesus dismisses the notion that we should pat ourselves on the back for being kind and loving toward anyone who behaves likewise. According to Him, that's a given. When others treat us well, of course we should treat them well too. But what about when people aren't so loving and kind? What do we do then?

> But love your enemies, and do good, and lend, expecting nothing in return, and your reward will be great, and you will be sons of the Most High, for he is kind to the ungrateful and the evil. Be merciful, even as your Father is merciful (Luke 6:35-36, *ESV*).

Whenever the way we live becomes an obstacle to the message of the hope of Christ, we need to make a change. If we aren't being merciful, we aren't being like the One we claim to serve. People need to see Jesus in us. Wherever Jesus went, He transformed individual lives and entire communities. His life sent waves through the sea of time. And His life was marked by kindness.

Cultivating Kindness

The issue of kindness isn't new for Christians. Apparently, it's been a topic worthy of teaching and training since the early days of the Church. The apostle Paul spent plenty of time urging new believers to be kind to others:

> Be kind to one another, tenderhearted, forgiving one another, as God in Christ forgave you (Eph. 4:32, *ESV*).

It sounds great and wonderful. "Sign me up!" you might say. Most of us want to be kinder toward others, but how exactly do we do that? What marks a heart of kindness?

Recognize people as precious children of God. When we are unkind toward others, we dehumanize them, reducing them to a pile of offenses. That's how it becomes so easy to be unkind. *They* don't have feelings. *They* are vile beings who are ruining our happiness. *They* deserve to suffer. But if you take this stance toward someone who has hurt or offended you, you are alone in the way you feel. God doesn't feel this way toward that person. Jesus didn't feel that way toward those who shredded His flesh with a vicious flogging and hammered nails through His hands to hang Him from a cross. Instead of being what we would consider justifiably angry at such undeserved treatment, Jesus said this: "Father, forgive them" (Luke 23:34).

I (Jason) don't have any problem being kind to my daughters when they destroy something in my house. Sure, I'm disappointed that they dropped my wife's phone in a cup of water and ruined it, or I feel frustrated that they decided to play beauty salon and cut each other's hair. My wife and I enact disciplinary measures in response to their general mischief, but at no point do I choose to be unkind to them. I see them as precious children—my precious children—and recognize that they need grace, not rage.

Consciously looking at others in this way is a great place to start when cultivating a heart of kindness. It's a great way to reflect the heart of Jesus.

Be full of grace, quick to forgive. We may not consider ourselves "mean" per se, but we have no problem holding a grudge until we feel like the offending person's debt has been satisfied. They need to know they can't do *that* to us anymore—so we lock them up in our mind's imaginary prison, refusing to let them out until the end of the sentence we have imposed. The lengths we go to in order to complete this punishment can come across as unkind, not to mention that this sort of behavior is not even close to how God would have us act.

For Jesus, there was no offense against Him so great that He couldn't forgive the offender. His approach toward sinners infuriated the religious people of His day, but He was unwavering in the way He loved people and extolled forgiveness.

As Jesus passed on from there, he saw a man called Matthew sitting at the tax booth, and he said to him, "Follow me." And he rose and followed him. And as Jesus reclined at table in the house, behold, many tax collectors and sinners came and were reclining with Jesus and his disciples. And when the Pharisees saw this, they said to his disciples, "Why does your teacher eat with tax collectors and sinners?" But when he heard it, he said, "Those who are well have no need of a physician, but those who are sick. Go and learn what this means, 'I desire mercy, and not sacrifice.' For I came not to call the righteous, but sinners" (Matt. 9:9-13, *ESV*).

Jesus desired mercy. You can't be merciful without being kind. The way that Jesus embodied mercy rattled the religious leaders. Matthew was scum in their eyes, yet here Jesus was, hanging out with him. With Jesus, Matthew's past was instantly wiped clean, irrelevant—forgiven. Matthew made his living by taking advantage of fellow Jews, requiring—with authority—whatever extra money they had. This kind of extortion is likely far worse than most of the offenses that stir us to treat others in an unkind manner; so when we're faced with those lesser challenges, we would do well to remember Jesus' model of how to extend grace and mercy.

When we show people kindness, we present them with a clearer image of the heart of Jesus. Instead of Christians being repulsive, suddenly they appear attractive. No one wants to join a group of people who are corporately unkind, but when someone encounters a person marked by kindness, he or she wants to draw near and learn the secret. "How can you be so unbothered when people do wrong to you?" the inquirer demands to know. "Why don't you get revenge?" When you answer truthfully about how God transformed—and continues to transform—your life, you pave the way for His kindness to lead the seeker to repentance as well.

Chapter 5

THE EXCLUSIVE-INCLUSIVE CLUB

Exclusive → Inclusive

> *He drew a circle that shut me out—*
> *Heretic, rebel, a thing to flout.*
> *But love and I had the wit to win:*
> *We drew a circle that took him in.*
>
> Edwin Markham

I (Jason) will never forget the early spring day when four classmates grabbed my scrawny 11-year-old body and pulled my appendages in every direction while a fifth classmate repeatedly punched me in the stomach. The assault only lasted about a minute, and then my assailants dropped me on my back on top of a gravel pile. That night, between sobs, I told my parents I never wanted to go back to that school again. A week later, I took a test to enroll at a school on the other side of town—the largest private school in the state of South Carolina.

Through recreational sports programs, I knew plenty of the kids who attended the school. But I had no idea what I was walking into—an elite private school that wasn't exactly accepting of my kind. By my kind, I mean the not-so-wealthy kind. My dad was planting a church, and my mom was home-schooling my siblings. A poor, homeschooling family? I had two strikes against me before I even introduced myself—and you can believe that everybody who was anybody knew I didn't live in an upscale neighborhood, thanks to the school's furiously churning gossip mill.

My Walmart brand clothes and lack of knowledge regarding pop music ensured that I was ostracized almost immediately. Every day, my loving father inched through the parking lot with me in our 1979 Honda Civic hatchback, joining a parade of BMWs, Jaguars and foreign sports cars. Each time we pulled into the parking lot, I once again felt out of place. The resident bullies got their mornings off to a roaring start by reminding me of my misfit status before I even took 10 steps toward the building. I endured so much teasing that I started to wonder which was worse—the physical abuse I had endured at my previous school or the mental abuse I was suffering now. Being in middle school is hard enough; the fact that I didn't fit neatly into the status quo compounded my misery.

Just because I was present at school with my classmates in no way meant I was included in their groups. I didn't receive invitations to birthday parties. No one asked me to sit with him or her at lunch. I went to our school's football games with my dad, but I was never asked to participate in the raucous two-hand touch games that took place behind the stands. In every way imaginable, I was an outsider.

Then I met Pinckney.

I knew who Pinckney was from playing baseball in our city league, but I didn't really like him from afar. He was 12 years old and threw a nasty curve ball—and every coach I knew said if you threw a curve ball before you turned 14 you would ruin your arm. I didn't want to ruin my arm, but Pinckney didn't seem to care—and his curve ball was unhittable. I was insanely jealous. He was also the kind of player who clapped and yelled at the opposing pitcher, getting in his head and eventually causing him to lose focus and make a mistake.

But when he wasn't throwing curve balls or displaying a spirited competitive nature, he went to my new school. When I met Pinckney at school, my opinion of him changed. He was very popular with our entire class, particularly the girls, who swooned when he talked to them. But he didn't seem to care about what people thought of him. Or what kind of clothes he wore. Or any other superficial matter. He was outspoken, yet compassionate. He was completely respected and very much included by our classmates, yet he didn't care to exclude anyone. He was different.

I realized just how different he was when he asked me if I wanted to spend the night at his house. *Me? Why does he like me?* I wondered. I had no idea, but I needed a friend. Could I possibly become friends with one of the most popular kids in my class?

I went over to Pinckney's house, and it was just like almost everyone else's in my class—spacious and located near the local country club. He wore nice clothes, and his family had nice cars—you know, all those things that *seem* important when you're in middle school, especially when you don't have them. But that's not what we talked about when we hung out. We didn't talk about stuff—we talked about life and baseball. Sometimes, we even talked about girls. I began to feel included.

Despite Pinckney's general popularity, he had a relatively small inner circle of close friends—and suddenly, I was in it. While not all of his friends were as removed from concern about superficial things as Pinckney was, they were a group of guys who cared more about each other than they did about looking cool. That was the beginning of a friendship that remains strong after 25 years. It's hard to imagine how I would've managed going to school there without Pinckney and the way he included me.

When I reflect on this period in my life, I recognize a valuable lesson: People don't feel included by being invited to an event—they feel included when you invite them into your life. This is what made Pinckney so different. I watched him continue to welcome outsiders into his circle whenever new kids transferred to our school. Later, I watched him practice inclusivity on his rural farm, treating poor farmhands like they were as important as the president. Driving around with him on his farm and talking with him about the men who worked for him, I was always amazed at just how much Pinckney knew about them. He knew their kids' names and could tell you some interesting stories about each worker. It was easy to see that Pinckney had invited them all in.

An Invitation to "Church"

As Christians, we need to redefine what we mean by the word "church." Instead of using the term to refer to a physical building or a specific Sunday-morning service, we need to explain that we're talking about a collection of believers. Making this distinction will help us in our efforts to reflect the heart of Jesus, who was incredibly inclusive. When we ask people to come to a meeting in a building, we're not exactly fostering an environment of inclusiveness; inviting them into our lives is how we include people.

That's not to say there's anything wrong with inviting people to church. Regularly, I (Tri) encourage people to bring their friends to church with them. Our teaching team makes it a goal to present the truth with simplicity each Sunday. We are keenly aware that this just might be the only time someone darkens the doors of a church. It might be the first—or the last—chance they've decided to give church. It is our responsibility to share the truth, making room for the Holy Spirit to convict them and draw them to God's love.

But that in and of itself doesn't make a church inclusive. The invitation to dinner and the eventual revelations about who you are and what God has done in your life are the kinds of things that create an environment of inclusivity. If we are adamant about the fact that the Church is actually people and not a building (as evidenced by the explosive growth of house churches in China), then being inclusive starts with us.

The Inclusive Heart of Jesus

Our email inboxes get filled with invitations all the time. Requests for our presence at graduations, baby showers, baptisms, sporting events, weddings, a friend's band performance at a local club, an art show, and multi-level marketing demonstrations inundate us. If we accepted every invitation, we would spend the majority of our evenings and weekends attending events and parties. But we don't always go. Oftentimes, we don't even respond.

Sometimes, though, we do respond with a *yes* and make an effort to go. What's the difference? In many cases, it depends on how close we are to the person—and if the invitation is extended in person. If it's someone new, we respond positively because we are drawn to that person, couple or group of people and desire to get to know them better. We

believe the invitation we've received is going to lead to the opportunity for that to happen.

Jesus gave us some great examples of how to be inclusive.
His whole life was about extending an invitation to anyone
who would accept it.

> Jesus entered Jericho and was passing through. A man
> was there by the name of Zacchaeus; he was a chief tax
> collector and was wealthy. He wanted to see who Jesus
> was, but being a short man he could not, because of
> the crowd. So he ran ahead and climbed a sycamore-
> fig tree to see him, since Jesus was coming that way.
>
> When Jesus reached the spot, he looked up and
> said to him, "Zacchaeus, come down immediately. I
> must stay at your house today." So he came down at
> once and welcomed him gladly.
>
> All the people saw this and began to mutter, "He
> has gone to be the guest of a 'sinner.'"
>
> But Zacchaeus stood up and said to the Lord,
> "Look, Lord! Here and now I give half of my posses-
> sions to the poor, and if I have cheated anybody out
> of anything, I will pay back four times the amount."
>
> Jesus said to him, "Today salvation has come to
> this house, because this man, too, is a son of Abraham.
> For the Son of Man came to seek and to save what was
> lost" (Luke 19:1-10).

Jesus invited Himself over to Zacchaeus's house—and it
was scandalous. The religious leaders of the day struggled with
how such a "holy man" as Jesus could dine with a "sinner" like
Zacchaeus. In His response to the Pharisees' objections, Jesus'
not-so-subtle point is made: Deep and meaningful connec-

tions are forged when we invite people to meet us in a place devoid of religiosity—a place such as a home. Zacchaeus wasn't exactly seeking the truth in the synagogue. Why would he? Governed by the self-righteous Pharisees, the synagogue was a place where people were taught to ostracize him, relegating him to bottom-feeder status in their society. Not exactly a warm and welcoming environment.

Instead of inviting Zacchaeus to come and hear Him preach, Jesus suggested getting together at Zacchaeus's house. Instead of dragging Zacchaeus to a place that would inevitably remind him of all his shortcomings, Jesus went with Zacchaeus to a place where they were free to talk about a preferred future. Instead of rejecting the short, vindictive tax collector, Jesus welcomed him with open arms. When we see something that captivates us, we want to get closer to it. What Zacchaeus saw was the heart of Jesus—and he couldn't take his eyes off Him. He wanted to hear more of what Jesus had to say. This unconventional Teacher's refreshing words were irresistible to the parched soul stumbling through the desert.

That's what our faith should look like to the world when we walk it out the same way Jesus did. We should reflect the heart of Jesus in such a way that people are drawn to us, not repulsed by us. Hurting, isolated people crave that love and acceptance found so powerfully in a community of Christians who mirror the Messiah. Jesus strayed away from spending all His time with the "perfect" people—He went after the downcast, the outcast, the castoffs. But even then, it was less about a person's appearance or standing in society and more about the situation of his or her heart. Whenever people held onto a flicker of hope that their lives could be different, Jesus invited them to engage with Him as He fanned their flames into a roaring fire.

The Initiated Understood

For all the bewildered looks and confused responses the disciples gave Jesus after many of His messages, the Bible also takes note of when they understood the heart of Jesus and what He was doing. Throughout the majority of the four Gospels, it seems like Jesus' disciples were just stumbling along. There are so many stories that feature them scratching their heads and wondering what Jesus meant that it's easy to think that somehow Jesus had assembled a group of slow learners. But then there are those times when they didn't need an explanation of what Jesus was doing. They just knew.

One such moment is described in John 4—the story of Jesus talking with the woman at the well in Samaria. The Jews and the Samaritans didn't exactly get along; sometimes they even had violent conflicts. But there Jesus was, looking for a drink on a hot day and requesting water from a Samaritan woman. It's an interesting story, sandwiched between the accounts of one inquiring religious leader who approached Jesus under the cloak of night and an open inquisition by a group of religious leaders who challenged Jesus for healing someone on the Sabbath. Jesus was thirsty—but He knew the woman's thirst for the truth was greater. In a short conversation, she was rapt by His wisdom, knowledge and accepting heart. Jesus included her by sharing His big secret with her—He was the Messiah.

Then we come across this little nugget of information:

> Just then his disciples returned and were surprised to find him talking with a woman. But no one asked, "What do you want?" or "Why are you talking with her?" (John 4:27).

"But no one asked." Why did John feel this was so important to include? Maybe he wanted history to record that Jesus' disciples weren't slow all the time. Or maybe they were slow all the time—but *this* is something they got right away. Jesus exhibited inclusiveness in everything He did. He went through a place Jews often avoided and talked with a woman Jews were encouraged to ignore. His conversation with her undoubtedly transformed the trajectory of this woman's life. Like the Jews, she was expecting a Messiah—someone to rescue her from the dismal life she was leading. The parade of men, one after another. The endless quest for meaningful love. The need to feel appreciated and beautiful. Many Jews refused to accept Jesus as the Messiah because they wanted something else—a political savior, perhaps. But not the woman at the well. The thing she wanted from the Messiah was exactly what Jesus offered. He was an accepting conduit of God's love—a Messiah who was only interested in her past so He could heal her of it to ensure a brighter future.

No one asked, because they knew. They had all been there, sitting on the outside, excluded from the crowds and places that everyone aspired to join and go, respectively. And then they had met Jesus. He didn't brow beat them for their sinful ways. He didn't lose His patience with them. He committed to spending His life with them and showing them the way to live—a way that brings true life.

"Come and See"

When we come across as exclusive in the way we handle those who don't profess to follow Jesus, we fail to reflect the character of Christ. Unfortunately, it's easy to replace God's grace with a sense of entitlement to salvation after we have been Christians for a while. We get lulled into thinking that as we follow God and become godlier people, we should get into heaven because of what we do. We deserve it, right? We gave up everything to follow Jesus—and as a result, we're better than all those people who haven't done that yet. It sounds silly when we say it that way, but that's an attitude that is characteristic of exclusive Christianity.

To avoid exclusivity in the way we live out our faith, we must take a closer look at the way Jesus invited those closest to Him into His life.

> The next day John was there again with two of his disciples. When he saw Jesus passing by, he said, "Look, the Lamb of God!"
>
> When the two disciples heard him say this, they followed Jesus. Turning around, Jesus saw them following and asked, "What do you want?"
>
> They said, "Rabbi" (which means Teacher), "where are you staying?"
>
> "Come," he replied, "and you will see."
>
> So they went and saw where he was staying, and spent that day with him. It was about the tenth hour.
>
> Andrew, Simon Peter's brother, was one of the two who heard what John had said and who had followed Jesus. The first thing Andrew did was to find his brother Simon and tell him, "We have found the Messiah" (that is, the Christ). And he brought him to Jesus.
>
> Jesus looked at him and said, "You are Simon son of John. You will be called Cephas" (which, when translated, is Peter) (John 1:35-42).

This story runs squarely against the grain of Christian culture today. If these events were to play out in the twenty-first century, they likely wouldn't end with an invitation to follow the young rising pastor and see how he lives life, but rather with an encouragement to follow him on Twitter and check out his podcasts on iTunes. Even within the Church, we have become more enamored with what people say than how they live. Frankly, many people seem not to care how pastors live, as long as the sermons are interesting and entertaining. Maintain that platform and sell lots of books. We have traded character for the cult of celebrity.

That's not how Jesus did it. The Son of God knew that the best way to include people—and to find out if they were serious about following Him—was to invite them into His life. Of course, Jesus did not have a busy nationwide tour to conduct or a large ministry to run. But everyone's time is precious, and Jesus knew that His was short. Still, He gave the two inquiring disciples an intimate look at His life. They in turn were so taken with Jesus that they began recruiting people to bring to Him. Interestingly enough, this was before Jesus' first miracle—so something else about the way He lived His life must have been compelling.

F. B. Meyer observes:

Notice how our Lord develops men. He invites them to his familiar friendship—"Come and see," and he looks deep down into their hearts, detecting capacities and possibilities that were hidden even from themselves, but which he helps them to realize: "Thou shalt be called Cephas," a "rock."

In our fast-paced world, we sometimes forget that putting the time and effort into truly seeing the people around us is well worth the investment. When people feel understood, appreciated and welcomed into community, barriers begin to crumble and opportunities for meaningful relationship and growth arise.

Jesus was inclusive because He came for everyone, not just a select few. Why exclude anyone if that's your heart? Why leave out one soul? Why not be the most inclusive person ever to walk the earth?

Brennan Manning takes note of Jesus' inclusiveness in *The Ragamuffin Gospel*:

> [Jesus'] love for failures and nobodies was not an exclusive love—that would merely substitute one class prejudice for another. He related with warmth and compassion to the middle and upper classes not because of their family connections, financial clout, intelligence, or Social Register status, but because they, too, were God's children.[1]

This point must not be lost among Christians today. While the Church has made great strides in focusing more on serving the poor, it must not treat the wealthy with disdain. In God's economy, we're all poor and all desperately in need of a Savior. The homeless guy in a gutter and the rich banker in a mountainside mansion both need to experience God's redeeming love. Jesus is an equal opportunity Savior. If you come as you are, He will invite you to come and see life in a new way—a way that will leave you transformed.

The Imperfect Picture

The proposition of inviting people into our lives might be scary for some. Handwringing. Angst. Fear. This is how many of us react when we realize the curtain is about to be opened on our lives and everyone will see us for who we truly are. Will they see a fraud? A pretender? A wannabe? Our hands grip the edge of the curtain to keep it securely in place. *Nobody wants to see back here.*

For years, I (Jason) was afraid of what people might see if they took a peek at my heart. I feared it would turn into an FBI-type raid on my soul, complete with prospecting friends carrying out boxes of evidence that would seal my fate. *Christian? Yeah, right. More like hypocrite and phony.* At least, that's how I imagined the conversation going. That's what happens when your idea of following Jesus is reduced to strict adherence to rules instead of being expanded to a transformative journey of relationship with Jesus.

It's hard to pretend to be someone you're not. Working tirelessly to project an image of having it all together and knowing all the answers will wear a person out. Eventually, you have to come clean. Surprisingly, that's where the real fun begins.

People don't expect us to be perfect—not even non-Christians. In many cases, we are our own toughest critics, rehashing our daily actions and wondering why we can't change. Instead of allowing the Holy Spirit to continue the redemptive work already started in us, we wrestle away the reins of our lives in an attempt to go at the pace we think is best. Sometimes, we're cracking the whip, all too unaware that we're tied to a post outside the stable. We want to move forward, forgetting that God's plan for our lives rarely matches our own. We don't envision the brokenness that it takes to help us become more like Jesus. Instead, we simply want the end product—and we want it now.

However, inviting people into our lives and allowing them to see us in process can be freeing—for both us *and* the people we invite in. I once had a friend who was convinced I never did anything wrong. He frequently mentioned how "perfect" I was—how I never got upset, and nothing seemed to bother me. Then he saw me in action one night. He walked in the door of my apartment about the time that I became unglued over a sophomoric prank a neighbor was pulling on me. I saw a glint of fear in his eyes over what I might do that eventually faded to a smirk. "I've never seen you act like that before," he said once the fracas subsided.

Before I had a chance to explain or justify my anger (and unrighteous response), he chuckled and added, "I didn't realize you were so normal."

Hearing those words, my first response was to be upset at myself for failing to control my temper and handle the situation with just a smidge of Christian maturity. But then I realized how my friend was processing what he had just seen: *That guy loves Jesus a bunch, but he's not perfect. Maybe I can do this, too.*

When we invite people into our lives, there is the chance that things can get messy. But it can be a beautiful mess. In a moment when I thought I had chunked my witness to my friend out the window, I saw my imperfection become a point of connection with him. Suddenly, he could relate to me much better. That night we had a great conversation over a plate of scattered, covered and smothered hash browns at the Waffle House. I shared with him some of my abysmal failures when it came to reflecting the heart of Jesus. He already knew I wasn't perfect, so there was no use trying to prop up some image I thought others wanted to see—especially when I realized that what my friend really wanted to see was how I responded when I knew I had fallen short.

Being authentic when we include others powerfully reflects the heart of Jesus. We don't have it all together yet, but we're committed to walking out our faith. Sometimes we get it right; other times we don't. But we'll always get it right when we make others feel welcome and help them realize that the faith we have is just as accessible to them as it is to us.

Becoming Inclusive

The very nature of God's redemptive plan is that it *is* inclusive: "For God so loved *the world* . . ." That's not "world" in the spherical orb-shaped sense; it's people God loves and people He sent Jesus to die for. For that reason, we need to resist the urge to retreat to our conclaves of faith and we must be bolder in the ways we include others.

Step out in faith. How willing are we to step out in faith for Jesus? Oftentimes we are given opportunities to proclaim the name of Jesus by looking at a dismal circumstance and trusting that God will change it despite its appearance. But are we bold enough to go forth with this when these situations arise in our lives?

Consider the story of Peter and John and their encounter with the lame beggar outside the temple gate:

> One day Peter and John were going up to the temple at the time of prayer—at three in the afternoon. Now a man crippled from birth was being carried to the temple gate called Beautiful, where he was put every day to beg from those going into the temple courts. When he saw Peter and John about to enter, he asked them for money. Peter looked straight at him, as did John. Then Peter said, "Look at us!" So the man gave them his attention, expecting to get something from them.
>
> Then Peter said, "Silver or gold I do not have, but what I have I give you. In the name of Jesus Christ of

Nazareth, walk." Taking him by the right hand, he
helped him up, and instantly the man's feet and ankles became strong. He jumped to his feet and began
to walk. Then he went with them into the temple
courts, walking and jumping, and praising God. When
all the people saw him walking and praising God, they
recognized him as the same man who used to sit begging at the temple gate called Beautiful, and they were
filled with wonder and amazement at what had happened to him (Acts 3:1-10).

There was nothing special about this day, as Peter and
John headed to the temple for prayer at the standard time. But
just in the way they carried themselves, it was obvious a dramatic transformation had occurred in their lives. Peter, who
had denied Christ three times before the rooster crowed, was
now proclaiming the power of the resurrection to anyone who
would listen—and to many who wouldn't.

As Peter and John neared the temple, they came across a
lame man who sat outside the gates, begging for money. The
man had been begging there his whole life, so Peter undoubtedly had seen him more than once. But on this particular
morning, Peter decided that walking by one more time without giving the man anything wouldn't suffice—it was time to
step out in faith.

He didn't invite the lame beggar to church (although that
would have been bold in itself, since the law precluded the
man from coming inside, as his disability made him "un-
clean"). No, Peter invited him to so much more:

Taking him by the right hand, he helped him up, and
instantly the man's feet and ankles became strong.

He jumped to his feet and began to walk. Then he went with them into the temple courts, walking and jumping, and praising God (vv. 7-8).

The Bible mentions nothing about the state of the lame man's soul. Who knows if he believed Jesus was the Messiah? Who knows if he just sat outside the temple begging because he thought it was the best place to make money? That wasn't the point of the story. No longer could the lame man deny the power of God, as he went walking and leaping and declaring God's name in the temple. The man's healing not only set him to dancing, but it also set the entire temple to praising God. All this started with Peter deciding to step out in faith and invite this man to experience Jesus and the kingdom of God.

Be attentive to the voice of the Holy Spirit. Deep down in our hearts, we know it is the Lord. His soft, gentle voice is urging us to do something . . . but we're not quite sure we want to do it. What God is asking us to do seems a little bit silly or out of the ordinary. Still, whether or not we are comfortable with what He is telling us, we know we need to obey. The Holy Spirit is asking us to include someone—to help them experience God's power in a fresh way.

Consider Philip's experience as he walked along a desert road leading to Gaza:

Now an angel of the Lord said to Philip, "Go south to the road—the desert road—that goes down from Jerusalem to Gaza." So he started out, and on his way he met an Ethiopian eunuch, an important official in charge of all the treasury of Candace, queen of the Ethiopians. This man had gone to Jerusalem to worship, and on his way home was sitting in his chariot reading the book of Isaiah the prophet. The Spirit told Philip, "Go to that chariot and stay near it."

Then Philip ran up to the chariot and heard the man reading Isaiah the prophet. "Do you understand what you are reading?" Philip asked. . . .

The eunuch asked Philip, "Tell me, please, who is the prophet talking about, himself or someone else?" Then Philip began with that very passage of Scripture and told him the good news about Jesus.

As they traveled along the road, they came to some water and the eunuch said, "Look, here is water. Why shouldn't I be baptized?" And he gave orders to stop the chariot. Then both Philip and the eunuch went down into the water and Philip baptized him (Acts 8:26-30,34-38).

Philip's ministry was growing rapidly. He was becoming a powerful evangelist, not because of how convincing he was with his words, but because of how attentive he was to the voice of the Lord. As he served the Lord and communicated the heart of God to all who would listen, amazing signs and wonders accompanied his teaching. People began following him.

So, we can imagine that when Philip heard the Holy Spirit leading him elsewhere—down a desert road leading to Gaza—he was somewhat perplexed. Why would the Lord take him out of a place of great impact? Wouldn't it be impossible to make as many strides for the kingdom of God on this road? How could he invite anyone to experience God out here in the middle of the desert?

An important element in learning to be inclusive like Jesus is surrendering ourselves to Him in such a way that wherever He calls us, whenever He calls us, we will be obedient and go.

This is what Philip did. The bold obedience that manifested itself in Philip's encounter with the Ethiopian eunuch started well before he arrived alongside the man's chariot—it started when Philip began walking down that long desert road.

In our own walks with the Lord, we must be attentive to the Holy Spirit speaking to us. That is the beginning of obedience. Before we can act according to God's will, we must get a clear picture of what He wants us to do. For Philip, that picture started with walking down a desert road with no promise of what he would find there.

As it turned out, what he found was an opportunity to share Christ with a hungry man—a man who could influence an entire nation. The Ethiopian eunuch was so excited about what he had learned about Jesus that they stopped near some water and Philip baptized him. The Holy Spirit is our guide to lead us into the places where God desires for us to be. In those places, we meet the people Jesus calls us to include in His kingdom.

Jesus said, "When the Counselor comes, whom I will send to you from the Father, the Spirit of truth who goes out from the Father, he will testify about me. And you also must testify, for you have been with me from the beginning" (John 15:26-27). As we listen to the voice of the Holy Spirit in our lives, we will have opportunities to be used in ways that we never imagined—ways that might even change an entire nation from a desert road.

Inclusion doesn't equal convenience. We may recognize an opportunity to include someone, but we just don't feel like doing it. Maybe it's late or we're supposed to be somewhere shortly—for whatever reason, we don't respond. We assume that if the Lord really wants us to talk to that person, the opportunity will arise again later, and we go on with our lives. We begin to walk away—even though the Lord is still tugging at our hearts to speak to the person He's put before us.

Sitting chained in a prison cell with Silas, Paul might have thought that his situation was not conducive to sharing the Lord with those around him. Unable to write or talk with the other prisoners, Paul and Silas resorted to spreading the gospel through song. As the two began to sing of the wonders of their Lord, the foundations of the prison began to shake—until they were shaken loose.

Shouts of joy rang throughout the prison as inmates broke toward the door for freedom. Paul and Silas were undoubtedly caught up in the moment, rejoicing that the Lord had provided a way out of this unjust situation for them. What a relief to know that the God of the universe was looking out for them!

But even as their own freedom beckoned, Paul and Silas saw one man still imprisoned—the jailer. At midnight, the jailer had been asleep—until the shaking of the jail and opening of the jail cells woke him. He arose to discover all his prisoners fleeing to freedom . . . and there was nothing he could do to stop them. He knew that rebuke from his superiors was inevitable, even though the situation was beyond his control. Shame would be heaped upon his head—and they might just kill him for his apparent act of irresponsibility.

Paul set aside his open invitation to physical freedom and turned his attention toward bringing eternal freedom to a man held in spiritual bondage. This may not have seemed like the ideal moment to pause and share the gospel with the jailer, but it was evident to Paul that the dire circumstances called for action.

The jailer woke up, and when he saw the prison doors open, he drew his sword and was about to kill himself because he thought the prisoners had escaped. But

Paul shouted, "Don't harm yourself! We are all here!" The jailer called for lights, rushed in and fell trembling before Paul and Silas. He then brought them out and asked, "Sirs, what must I do to be saved?" (Acts 16:27-30).

Before the night was over, the jailer and his entire family were saved. By the next morning, so was his life, as the magistrates realized what a terrible injustice had been performed against Paul and Silas, two Roman citizens.

Part of being an inclusive Christian means sacrificing our desires for the moment in an effort to make an eternal impact. When we find ourselves willing to lay aside our lives for just a small period of time in order to reach someone who is struggling or hungry for what God has to offer, we discover that God can use us in powerful ways.

Chapter 6

THE HEART
OF A PHARISEE

Self-righteous → Grace-filled

Do not let any unwholesome talk come out of your mouths,
but only what is helpful for building others up according to their
needs, that it may benefit those who listen.

Ephesians 4:29

When I (Jason) was attending the University of Georgia, I had a group of friends who considered it their Christian duty to preach from the open-air free speech platform. On any given Friday afternoon, one of my friends could be heard passionately sharing the gospel and talking about God's love. Before they went, they always tried to rally others to attend. I think it was an effort to lessen the verbal abuse as much as it was to offer moral support. But why would you need such support in a free-thinking collegiate environment? In short, "turn-or-burn" guy.

You may not know the particular turn-or-burn guy I'm referencing, but you've experienced someone like him in your life. You've cringed when a loud and obnoxious person began shouting judgmental things at passersby, using his or her soapbox to assert a moral superiority and condemn everyone else. The street-corner evangelist I knew would sometimes wear a sandwich board, which described in great detail how every person within earshot was going to hell. How could I disassociate the way I sought Jesus from such an unloving and condemning person? Undoubtedly, the man on the corner would call himself a Christian, as would I. So the first connotation to pop into someone's head when I affirmed that I was a Christian involved all those traits demonstrated on the street corner by the so-called evangelist. People didn't think about the Jesus I claimed to follow—they thought about J.A.M.E.S. I found this upsetting, as did many of my friends.

Occasionally, turn-or-burn guy would be at the platform at the same time as one of my friends, but his appearances on other days of the week were what created a hostile environment. Everybody on campus was annoyed by the judgmental epithets he screamed at the top of his lungs. To say that he had not learned some of the more gentle ways to share the gospel would be a gross understatement. Some of my friends would linger near the platform while turn-or-burn guy was preaching in an effort to engage the man in a conversation. Maybe they hoped that they could appeal to him and have him step down from his literal soapbox—perhaps have a cup of coffee and discuss theological matters as well as issues of the heart. But it never happened. He would just get angrier and angrier, yelling louder and longer.

At first, we all saw a disturbed man who needed a hug. But the more offensive he got, the more challenging conversations about issues of faith became. Calling a young college co-ed wearing a short skirt a "whore of Babylon" wasn't exactly the way to engender goodwill and earn the right to be heard. Unfortunately, those who identified themselves as Christians were lumped in with turn-or-burn guy when it came to collective groupthink. So, we decided to "fix" him. We wanted to set him straight—dress him down in public. The angrier he got, the angrier we got. But our anger was righteous, right?

That's when Tom, our campus ministry pastor, challenged us to consider the motives of our hearts. "Why do you want to go down there?" he asked. "To show how spiritual you are? To win a public theological debate? Or do you want to go show him God's love?" Tom had an incredible knack for steering students down a path that was more Christlike, especially when they were careening toward a theological ditch. Loving people holds infinitely more value in God's kingdom than clever biblical arguments do. Tom's piercing question got to us. We stopped challenging turn-or-burn guy and started loving him. We were kind to him. Eventually, he stopped coming to the platform. We never really knew why. Maybe he thought his work was done, or maybe he was undone by love. Either way, he was gone, and an environment of civility regarding religion returned to the campus.

In our efforts to correct a Pharisee, we started to become one. Instead of extending grace toward this man—who was our Christian brother, whether we liked him or not—we offered him a rebuke and an argument. We thought that if we were trying to "protect" the name of God, then we could say whatever we want, especially when we knew we were *right*. However, even our best intentions go awry when held up to the light of Christ. Do we want to reflect Jesus or force others to act a certain way that we think Jesus would approve of? The former approach is always better.

What Is a Pharisee?

During Jesus' time on earth, Pharisees were religious leaders who were responsible for guiding a flock of followers. Pharisees pledged to devote themselves to Levitical purity and were part of their own brotherhood. They determined to separate themselves from the rest of the population by the way they lived their lives. As the Roman culture encroached on their sacred beliefs, they stood firm. Yet their commitment to uphold the law above all else created a fatal flaw that was revealed in the light of God's love and grace. The Pharisees looked perfect on the outside, but their piousness refused to make room for the Messiah. They had become accustomed to being the standard bearer for all things within the Jewish religious law—and Jesus threatened that power. The Pharisees should have been the ones heralding Jesus' arrival, letting every Jewish person know that the Messiah had indeed come. He was here! But power trumped truth, and Jesus saw right through them. As a result of Jesus' characterization of Pharisees, they have become synonymous with self-righteousness. Sadly, that is how many people view Christians today.

Consider an example from our culture. A pastor with a huge platform and radio ministry speaks out against a certain sin. Two years later, we learn that this pastor was grappling with that same sin himself. It costs him his church. It costs him his reputation. It may even cost him his family. If you think we are referring to a certain pastor, you are mistaken. We wish that there were just *one* example of this in our culture. Instead, it's a narrative that applies to many pastors and leaders purporting to embody Christian values today. These types of occurrences hardly raise an eyebrow anymore, as they merely serve to reinforce an already widely held view. The pattern is not limited to well-known pastors. It happens to pastors of small churches, too—and to business executives and husbands and teachers and mothers. None of us is safe from adopting an air of superiority when it comes to our morals and values. Not only is such an attitude unloving, but it also tends to be short-lived. If we're not grounded in God's Word and in tune with His heart for us, we are as likely as anyone else to sell our morals and values down the river. No matter who we are, we are all susceptible to moments of weakness during which that part of us that's not yet fully sanctified caves in on itself.

However, self-righteousness is more than that. Self-righteousness is when we project what we believe to be un-equivocally right—and do it with a pious heart. *Look what we did to help the poor—all for Jesus' glory, of course.* We make a show out of how awesome and amazing we are—and how "perfect" our belief system is. *Our denomination is more theologically sound than yours.* There's no room for error in our thinking—and how dare anyone question anything that we say is the truth? *I am right, and if you don't agree with me, you're wrong. Those mainline denominationalists! Those post-modernists! Those emergents! Those Cath-olics! Those evangelicals!* Human beings can be self-righteous about anything. There are self-righteous atheists, self-righteous sports fans, self-righteous authors, self-righteous law enforce-ment officials. Anybody can adopt this type of attitude about anything—and be reluctant to relinquish it for fear of losing face, even when the evidence suggests something contrary to their beliefs.

The Pharisees embodied this definition of self-righteousness. They made public displays of their faith, just to show how holy they were. They went to great lengths to demonstrate their righteousness, heaping guilt on others who didn't choose to follow their lead. Jesus regularly rebuked them, mostly because He perceived the attitudes of their hearts. He wasn't judging them as much as He was challenging their tightly held belief that their brand of religion was above reproach. The truth is, all their rules weren't enough to help them live lives that were pleasing to God.

Author Philip Yancey explains how the Pharisees' self-righteousness, rooted in legalism, was destined to fail them:

> Legalism like the Pharisees' will always fail, not because it is too strict but because it is not strict enough. Thunderously, inarguably, the Sermon on the Mount proves that before God we all stand on level ground: murderers and temper-throwers, adulterers and lusters, thieves and coveters. We are all desperate, and that is in fact the only state appropriate to a human being who wants to know God. Having fallen from the absolute Ideal, we have nowhere to land but in the safety net of absolute grace.[1]

We all need God's grace, and as we seek to reflect the heart of Jesus rather than the heart of J.A.M.E.S., grace must be ever-present in the way we relate to others.

It's hardly fair to pick on the Pharisees from the perspective we have. We know that Jesus was the Messiah—and we know what He knew about the Pharisees' attitudes. From our position of 2,000 years of hindsight, mocking Jesus and questioning His motives seems ridiculous. But the Pharisees weren't convinced (or chose not to be for fear of losing their power)—and who knows if we would have been back then either. Not everyone was, so the chance that we all would have accepted Jesus' word as truth is not 100 percent.

Even when Nicodemus, a Pharisee, began to wonder if the whispers about Jesus being the Messiah were true, he still protected his self-image. In his exchange with Jesus under the cloak of night, Nicodemus showed that he was interested in

Jesus, but not in getting embarrassed like so many of his colleagues were when they openly confronted the Messiah. Read between the lines of what Nicodemus said:

> Rabbi, we know you are a teacher who has come from God. For no one could perform the miraculous signs you are doing if God were not with him (John 3:2).

In other words, *We know you're from God, but the Messiah? Really?* Everything else flew over the head of Nicodemus. He didn't understand the concept of being "born again." He didn't understand the idea of God's transforming power. Jesus appears to have been genuinely shocked at Nicodemus's ignorance. A spiritual leader who has no concept of what God's transforming a person looks like? Jesus didn't hold back from expressing His dismay. The encounter ends abruptly but not before Jesus launches into arguably the most popular Bible verse in the world: John 3:16. We're left to imagine Nicodemus slinking off into the shadows, reassured only by the notion that seeing Jesus alone at night had been a good decision. At least he didn't lose face with people and could still command followers. It was great to be a Pharisee—until Jesus came along.

Turning the Tables

We have all heard people make bold proclamations about what they will *never* do—only to watch them go on to do those very things. That's a symptom of a Pharisee—someone who is cocksure about his or her beliefs and moral system. This person *knows* that he or she will *never* do something. Oftentimes, that rhetoric is merely something that is repeated aloud to convince or remind oneself to choose another path when confronted with a choice deemed inappropriate. Nevertheless, the ensuing crash is often quite fiery, drawing both the disbelieving gawkers as well as the mocking masses.

Self-righteousness is a cancer, eating away at our hearts beneath the surface. In subtle ways, it erodes our reliance upon God and rests our wellbeing squarely upon our religious shoulders. Instead of depending on God, we trust in ourselves. Sometimes the change begins without so much as a visible ripple in our hearts, but the eventual tidal wave that sends our piety crashing down upon itself is devastating. While we often talk about self-righteousness as something we need to address, we don't always do so with the urgency and severity with which we might handle a disease like cancer.

The nineteenth-century Scottish preacher Robert Murray M'Cheyne didn't mince words when describing just how detrimental an attitude of self-righteousness can be to our hearts:

> Self-righteousness . . . is the largest idol of the human heart—the idol which man loves most and God hates most. Dearly beloved, you will always be going back to this idol. You are always trying to be something in yourself, to gain God's favour by thinking little of your sin, or by looking to your repentance, tears, prayers; or by looking to your religious exercises, your frames, etc.; or by looking to your graces, the Spirit's work in your heart. Beware of false Christs. Study sanctification to the utmost, but make not a Christ of it.[2]

God's redeeming love is what brings us into a true place of righteousness. If we're willing to be enveloped by His love, then we will experience true righteousness that a thousand lifetimes of determined holiness can't even touch. Being in right standing with God occurs when we move away from creating an idol of our holy behavior and begin accepting what it means to be loved by God—and what it means to show one another God's love.

The apostle Paul was one Pharisee who couldn't escape the long arms of God's love. Paul oversaw the stoning of Christians because they were not abiding by the law—at least, they were not abiding by the law as the Pharisees interpreted it. People feared Paul. He hid behind his religion as a way to ferret out those who dared to defy the religious leaders. But it all came crashing down one day. Blinded on the road to Damascus, Paul encountered God and was thrust into an intense time of discipleship. From that moment on, Paul's life was forever changed. The man who had dismissed Jesus as God's Son spent the rest of his life serving Him.

What's also noteworthy about Paul's conversion is how deep and transformative it was. He didn't just become a Christian and substitute one set of self-righteous rules for another. Instead, he valued only the Bible's laws, ridding himself of any allegiance to rules created by man—namely the Pharisees' laws. He didn't view God's law as something that bound him; rather, it was something that freed him. Then he used his vast experience as a self-righteous religious leader to challenge the Pharisees, who were still stuck in their legalistic ways of thinking. It was Paul's statement about the inclusive nature of the ministry to which God had called him that led to his ultimate undoing at the hands of the religious leaders:

> "When I returned to Jerusalem and was praying at the temple, I fell into a trance and saw the Lord speaking. 'Quick!' he said to me. 'Leave Jerusalem immediately, because they will not accept your testimony about me.'

" 'Lord,' I replied, 'these men know that I went from one synagogue to another to imprison and beat those who believe in you. And when the blood of your martyr Stephen was shed, I stood there giving my approval and guarding the clothes of those who were killing him.'

"Then the Lord said to me, 'Go; I will send you far away to the Gentiles.' "

The crowd listened to Paul until he said this. Then they raised their voices and shouted, "Rid the earth of him! He's not fit to live!" (Acts 22:17-22).

Surely people who claimed to be in tune with the heart of God would not turn into a mob, rioting for the death of a righteous man who sought to serve others and share the truth with them. But this crowd, led spiritually by Pharisees, did just that. The heart of the Pharisees' followers was leaking into the open. No grace or mercy was being expressed. Instead, in a gross display of self-righteousness, the crowd *knew* what was right—and that anyone who went against them needed to be silenced.

Paul went on to further demonstrate the vast chasm between the heart of the self-righteous and the heart of a humble follower of Jesus:

Paul looked straight at the Sanhedrin and said, "My brothers, I have fulfilled my duty to God in all good conscience to this day." At this the high priest Ananias ordered those standing near Paul to strike him on the mouth. Then Paul said to him, "God will strike you, you whitewashed wall! You sit there to judge me according to the law, yet you yourself violate the law by commanding that I be struck!"

Those who were standing near Paul said, "You dare to insult God's high priest?"

Paul replied, "Brothers, I did not realize that he was the high priest; for it is written: 'Do not speak evil about the ruler of your people.' "

Then Paul, knowing that some of them were Sadducees and the others Pharisees, called out in the Sanhedrin, "My brothers, I am a Pharisee, the son of a Pharisee. I stand on trial because of my hope in the resurrection of the dead" (Acts 23:1-6).

In a testy exchange, Paul called out the religious leaders for their hypocrisy and self-righteousness. He then apologized for insulting the religious ruler. But the only mercy Paul experienced was the result of a disagreement between the two factions of religious leaders. There was no repentance in response to Paul's words of truth. Instead of considering his assertion that they were acting self-righteously and behaving as hypocrites, they blasted Paul for his innocent insult. Self-righteousness vs. grace. A clearer contrast between those two character traits can't be found in the Bible.

Paul's experience serves as a model for us in a couple of ways. First, Paul shows us that *if we have a self-righteous heart, it can be changed.* If we allow God to work in our hearts, He can soften us in a way that we become transformed. No longer do we make it our mission to seek out and identify flaws in others. Instead, we extend grace toward others, keenly aware of where we came from and how we got to where we are now.

Second, this passage shows us that *humility is the antidote to self-righteousness.* When our righteousness is self-induced, we often don't realize it. We look at the rest of the world and wonder why others aren't as enlightened as we are. We think our faith is flawless and that others should be more like us in following Jesus' example. When we hear a sermon, we immediately wish so-and-so had been at church to hear it—but it's okay, because we'll tell him or her about it later. If this is starting to sound uncomfortably familiar—even if it's something that happens occasionally—we need to begin asking God to help us develop humility in our lives.

Humility begins by preferring others above ourselves and allowing for the possibility that we don't have all the answers—and in some cases, that we might even be wrong. This posture is incredibly helpful when engaging people in conversations about faith. Otherwise, we're going to be doing nothing more than preaching at them. If they're not attending church on a regular basis or at all, we can rest assured that they don't want to hear a sermon—they want to see practical demonstrations of faith.

Expose Your Self-righteousness

The problem with self-righteousness is that we don't always recognize just how much of it is in our lives. We are quick to recognize the trait in someone else, but in ourselves? Forget it. We would *never* act self-righteously, right? The truth is that self-righteousness is rampant in our society, and no matter how humble—how anti-self-righteous—we are, we can bet there is some deep-seated self-righteousness in there somewhere. Fortunately, there are ways to force our self-righteousness out into the open and deal with it. We must bring it to the surface before we can properly treat and diagnose this area of our hearts.

Challenge your preconceived ideas. Over the past few years, I (Jason) have grown quite fond of my atheistic and agnostic friends. In the past, I held them at arms' length, afraid I would not be able to answer all their tough questions and as a result might be the reason they never experienced a life-transforming moment with God. I knew I was right and they were wrong—

about pretty much everything—so why bother wasting my breath and precious time talking to them about the most central part of my life? But I decided to change my approach when I found myself holding lots of opinions about how atheists and agnostics thought and why they thought the way they did, yet never asking any of them about it. As I began to make an effort to engage non-Christian friends in conversation, I decided it was best for me primarily to ask questions and listen. That turned out to be a good move, as I discovered when many of them told me what usually happens when they have conversations about matters of faith: Christians shout them down and dismiss them.

Having been a member of my high school's debate team, I must admit that I enjoy a spirited debate. That's no secret to anyone who knows me. Engaging in conversations with others over controversial ideas gives me opportunity and motivation to pause and think about what I believe, even helping me to redefine or recast it in a way others can understand or relate to. While the foundation of my faith is concrete in God's Word, the ideas and opinions I form as to how faith is worked out on a daily basis remain in wet cement. No matter how strongly I feel that my idea is right or best, I have to leave open the possibility that maybe I'm wrong. I have discovered that adopting this attitude forces me to tread into these conversations with grace rather than with guns blazing.

My eclectic group of friends on Facebook makes that a dangerous place to host such conversations, but I do it anyway. Most of the time, the discussions are fantastic, with some interesting views put forth. There are occasions when I realize I've never even considered a person's point of view or thought about an issue from the perspective of his or her life experiences. As that friend shares, I (and others) gain valuable new

insights into the topic at hand. But then there are those days
when I cringe. A personal attack is launched—often by one of
my Christian friends against a non-Christian friend. The rhetoric gets amped up, and what was once a friendly debate suddenly devolves into a self-righteous diatribe. Sadly enough, it's
my atheistic friends who show the most restraint, walking
away first and being the more gracious people. If you're not
winsome and humble, you're not going to convince anyone
that you have an idea worth considering—even when truth is
on your side.

Get uncomfortable. It's easy to get smug in our righteousness if life remains comfortable all the time. In those moments
when we decide to stretch, we discover just how little we know
about the world around us—and God stokes our hearts to love
others in surprising ways.

I used to look the other way whenever I saw a homeless
man with his hand out, shaking his makeshift jar with coins
clanking around inside. In a glance, I could see how bloodshot
his eyes were. With a whiff, I could smell the stench of a brew-
ery emanating from his mouth between his pleas for my spare
change. Why would I want to perpetuate this type of behavior? I knew that if I gave him money, he wasn't going to spend
it on food but on more alcohol. He would sit on the street corner until people stopped giving him money—of that much I
was sure. So, I would do my part to help break the cycle—in all
my self-righteousness, I would look the other way. If I ignored
him and others did as well, perhaps he would sober up and get
his life together.

Then God convicted me. I started offering to buy a meal
for any homeless person who asked me for money for food.
But I would try not just to buy them food; instead, unless I
had a pressing matter to attend to, I would sit down and talk

with them, listening to their stories. This freed me from my poor attitude toward the homeless, helping me to realize that it was never just "a homeless person" standing on the corner, but a *person*—a person God loved.

Reaching out to people in need is not necessarily a natural thing for me. It's something that has to be nurtured—fostered in an environment of opportunity. After a while, I started making excuses for why I hadn't helped any homeless people lately: It was because I hadn't had any opportunities. But then I realized I hadn't had any opportunities because I hadn't been looking for any. I had drifted back into a complacent state regarding the homeless. I still had compassion for them, but I wasn't taking action. What I needed was to get uncomfortable and shake loose the self-righteousness that was creeping back in. For me, there's no better way to get out of my comfort zone than to spend time with my two gregarious daughters in public.

Nearing the end of a long, hot day carting my daughters around, I decided to take them to the toy store and reward them for an unprecedented day of obedience in public. Heeding a parent's every instruction for an entire day is an act to celebrate, particularly when the kids are ages three and four.

While I waited for a traffic light to turn green, my four-year-old daughter, Faith, looked out the window and asked the piercing question: "Daddy, what does that man's sign say?" I knew which man she was talking about. He stood six feet away from us, holding up a gut-wrenching sign:

Please help a vet. Jobless. Homeless. Hungry. God Bless.

The light changed, and I eased onto the accelerator while relaying the answer to her question and explaining what it meant.

"He doesn't have a job?" my daughter asked.

"That's what his sign says."

"Well, Daddy, you can give him your job."

I laughed nervously. "You can't just give someone your job, Faith. It's not that easy. And if I did, what would I do?"

"You could both do the job—then he could buy a house."

If only life were that simple. I didn't expect Faith to be satisfied with my response, but I plowed ahead anyway.

"It doesn't work like that, Faith." I knew what was coming next.

"He can stay with us."

By this point, I was wrestling with all kinds of issues—heart issues. I wanted to help, but I still had reservations. *Could I really let some stranger into my home?* It was a serious thought in my head, if only for a fleeting second. Before I could come to any comfortable resolution in my own mind, the little red-headed firecracker spouted off another suggestion, undaunted.

"Can we get him something to eat?" she asked.

That we could do. We drove to the nearest fast-food joint, purchased a hearty meal, and returned to deliver it to the man. I thought it was best that this unsuspecting guy get a full dose of the love coming from two half-pint girls with 10-gallon hearts. I also wanted the girls to realize that Christlike charity isn't about doing something to make a problem go away—it's about reaching out and being willing to stand with people in the midst of their most desperate moments in life.

We parked and began walking up the sidewalk toward the man standing at the corner.

I looked back at the two girls clamoring behind me: Faith was clinging to a giant soft drink, and Julia clutched a bag of food, both going to help a man in need of more than we could give him. It was pure innocence.

Moments later, we met Wiley. He had multiple sclerosis and a cane—but a grin that wouldn't go away. He looked at me and said, "You have your hands full with those heartbreakers." Before Wiley knew it, he had his hands full with the dinner my daughter had just persuaded me to buy for him.

"So you don't have a house?" Faith asked.

Wiley paused, shifting uncomfortably.

"No. No, I don't."

I held my breath. *Is Faith going to ask him to stay with us?* But she didn't say anything. She just looked up at him and grinned. After a few moments of surface conversation, I asked Wiley if we could pray for him before we left. I invited the perpetrator of this encounter to pray. Never shy about praying, in public or otherwise, Faith agreed.

"Dear God," she began, "thank You for Mr. Wiley. Will You give him a house—and when he goes into it, will You make sure it's filled with food? In Jesus' name, Amen."

It was a simple prayer, yet the kind that makes one tear up. There's nothing like the innocence of a child's prayer to dust the cobwebs off of a rusty heart and help it beat fresh again for others.

Jesus constantly challenged people's worldviews. Sometimes the challenge brought about change. Other times, people walked away from Him. No matter the outcome, Jesus always acted in love, approaching people from a place of humility and treating them with dignity.

Part III

BECOMING JESUS CHRISTIANS

Chapter 7

CARVE YOUR NAME ON HEARTS

Everybody can be great . . . because anybody can serve.
You don't have to have a college degree to serve. You don't have
to make your subject and verb agree to serve. You only need a
heart full of grace. A soul generated by love.

Dr. Martin Luther King, Jr.

If you spend any time in our church, you will quickly learn a few things about me (Tri). You will learn that I find joy in having seven points to every message. Aside from that being my favorite biblical number, seven points just make my messages feel complete. You will also discover that I believe Isaiah 61 is the blueprint for the Church to move forward and become relevant again in our culture, and that Romans 12 provides a detailed example of how we should live. You will also learn that the moment I felt confirmation in my spirit to go plant a church in Boise was when I found a yellow balloon in the Idaho wilderness containing a reference to 1 John 4:7-8 along with one simple message: "Let us love one another." No matter how nuanced and complex teaching God's Word might be at times, this simple phrase has a way of simplifying everything.

Throughout this book, we've shown you different perceptions people have of Christians and how we can change those ideas by becoming more like Jesus. When we exhibit Jesus' traits to the world around us, open hearts can't help but be drawn to the light and truth in us. People stop seeing us and start seeing Jesus. As Christians, that's all we can ever hope for—that we will allow God's deep transformative work to bring us to a place where we truly reflect Jesus in all that we do.

So how do we more clearly reflect Jesus?

What Is Love?

As we reach places in our journeys of faith where we realize there must be more to it than what we've experienced so far, we need to reassess the ways we are living. Those Christians who seem invigorated by their faith walks have found a secret. Except, it's not that big a secret; Jesus was quite open about it. The truth is, these people have discovered how to implement the direction that Jesus gave us in a life-changing way. When we strive to learn Jesus' big secret, we discover it laid out in two simple commands Jesus quoted when He responded to the question of which was the greatest commandment:

> "Love the Lord your God with all your heart and with all your soul and with all your mind and with all your strength." The second is this: "Love your neighbor as yourself." There is no commandment greater than these (Mark 12:30-31).

Love God with all that you are. Love your neighbor like you love yourself. It's simple and profound. The problem is that we struggle to understand the practical application of love. We know it when we see it, but we don't always know how to be loving.

The difficulty in trying to be loving is that we're often attempting to be something we're not. Since what flows out of our lives is what's in our hearts (see Prov. 4:23), we need to allow God to transform us at our cores. To embrace the kind of love that Jesus had—the kind of love that started a movement 2,000 years ago and is still going strong—we need far more than a behavior modification. What we need is to ask God to do this work in our hearts. We need Him to help us become patient, humble, kind, inclusive and grace-filled people—rather than judgmental, arrogant, mean-spirited, exclusive and self-righteous ones. We need the Holy Spirit to do the deep work in us that only He can do—and we need to give Him permission to do so.

Scripture gives us a simple litmus test to determine whether or not we are loving. The apostle Paul breaks it down like this:

> Love is patient, love is kind. It does not envy, it does not
> boast, it is not proud. It is not rude, it is not self-seeking,
> it is not easily angered, it keeps no record of wrongs.
> Love does not delight in evil but rejoices with the truth.
> It always protects, always trusts, always hopes, always
> perseveres. Love never fails (1 Cor. 13:4-8).

When I read this passage aloud at wedding ceremonies, I'm not sure that the people committing their lives to each other really understand the full implications of what Paul was saying. I know I didn't when I got married. If we're honest, we must admit that it takes time to grasp Paul's definition of love. Our understanding is sure to be dramatically different after years of marriage. We realize that love is less about a feeling and more about a deep commitment to a person—kind of like the way God commits Himself to us.

Dear friends, let us love one another, for love comes from God. Everyone who loves has been born of God and knows God. Whoever does not love does not know God, because God is love (1 John 4:7-8).

Jesus was love personified. He was all the things on Paul's list: patient, kind, humble, honorable, not self-seeking, slow to anger, forgiving, truthful, protecting, trusting, hoping, persevering, dependable. While walking on earth, Jesus demonstrated that there was a better way to live—a way less duty-bound to rules and more loving toward God and people. When men's rules clashed with loving people, love always won. No healing on the Sabbath? That was a rule made by man—a rule that Jesus determined was inappropriate at the time. A man needed to be healed, so Jesus showed him compassion—yet another trait of authentic love—by healing him.

Understanding the nature of love is important, but there comes a time, as the Lord begins to transform our hearts, when we must move beyond simple awareness of love and put it into action.

Love in Action

If we're going to take Jesus' charges seriously—the exhortations to love God, love people and make disciples—we must realize that sharing the intellectual head knowledge of faith is not enough when it comes to evangelism. It's important to have a good grasp of apologetics and be able to give deep and meaningful answers to questions like, "If God loves the world, why does He let so many bad things happen to good people?" But the skeptic can only be so convinced by clever rhetoric. What skeptics and other unbelievers really need is to see the *way* we love people according to Jesus' command. So here are seven questions you can ask yourself to help determine if the way you love people is the way Jesus loved people—and if you're really brave, you'll ask someone who knows you well to answer honestly for you.

1. Is Your Heart Broken Yet?

If you don't truly care about people, you will never get very far in your efforts to reflect the heart of Jesus. It's ground zero in the Christian life. While it may seem simple, it's a valid question. And we can't just care about some people—it has to be all of them. Jesus didn't die for a select few; He died for everyone. So our hearts need to break for all people's pain, suffering, loneliness and struggle.

Christian singer and songwriter Vicky Beeching writes some intensely intimate worship songs. It's clear from her lyrics that she desires to usher people into an encounter with God in worship. In an interview about how true worship extends far beyond congregational songs, Vicky related this interesting story about loving people and sharing your faith:

> My grandparents were missionaries to Israel first and then to Zimbabwe, Africa, for 20 years. I had the privilege when I was 10 years old to go out and spend a month with them in Zimbabwe. That was very formative for me as a child. It opened my eyes to so much of the suffering in the world. They told me that the gospel has to be preached not only in word but also in deed. You can't tell someone about Jesus if they're starving and you have food and they don't. So, it was a good formative experience for me as a worship leader because it reminded me that worship can't just be with words but it has to be with our lives.

The religious leaders in Jesus' day were interested in worshiping God through strict observance of the law. They were bent on mastering the outward appearance of serving God. But their hearts weren't broken for those around them. Compassion? They certainly didn't show any approaching the magnitude of Jesus' compassion. The only deeds the religious leaders were interested in doing were the ones prescribed by their strict Jewish law. Stopping to help a person because he or she needed help? Giving a thirsty person a drink? Demonstrating mercy instead of judgment? Those were distant afterthoughts in their minds. Conversely, those things were at the forefront of Jesus' mind. Having a broken heart for the world that translated into compassion was seminal to His message of "love God, love your neighbor."

Charles Spurgeon issued this challenge for us to live lives that demonstrate Christlike compassion:

> A good character is the best tombstone. Those who loved you, and were helped by you, will remember you when forget-me-nots are withered. Carve your name on hearts, and not on marble.[1]

It's easy to become apathetic regarding the state of everyone else's souls. We have our own souls to worry about—and, frankly, we're a mess. We boldly proclaim that we're going to put off evangelism until we can get our own acts together. The problem is, we're never truly going to get it all together. Thankfully, that's not really a prerequisite for loving others or sharing our faith as we share our lives. We need to do those things now. We need to love others furiously—so enveloping with the love of God that they are awakened to His presence in their lives. If our desire is to reflect Jesus, our brokenness for a broken world needs to have a profound influence on the way we live. Our compassion for a world dying without a Savior needs to trump any list conditions or other priorities we've created.

Nate Saint, a missionary pilot who was murdered—along with four other missionaries—by Auca Indians in the Amazon jungle in 1956, discovered that brokenness for the world around him. He knew he was risking his life when he set out to take the gospel to one of the fiercest tribes on the planet. But the conviction in the words he spoke just two weeks before he was martyred still rings out all these years later:

> As we have a high old time this Christmas may we who know Christ hear the cry of the damned as they hurtle headlong into the Christless night without ever a chance. May we be moved with compassion as our Lord was. May we shed tears of repentance for these we have failed to bring out of darkness. Beyond the smiling scenes of Bethlehem may we see the crushing agony of Golgotha.

What Saint and the other missionaries were doing was insane by the world's standards. They were trying to communicate the love of Jesus to a tribe that had been identified as one of the deadliest in the Amazon—and they didn't know the language or have a translator. But they weren't trying to impress anyone. They had all had their hearts broken for a people group who had never heard of Jesus.

When I (Jason) went to Ecuador with Mission Aviation Fellowship, nearly 65 years after Saint's death, I flew over the spot in the river where he was killed—and I talked with a member of the group that killed the missionaries. We didn't dwell on that moment, but we talked about what has transpired since—and what has happened has been nothing short of amazing. Dewey, who had become the elder tribe leader, was also the village's most senior pastor. I stood in the primitive church they had constructed, and we talked about how God had changed the entire destiny of this village. Now, the little church building was a hub for hosting gatherings of other village pastors throughout the region. It was the fruit of hearts broken for others—even others with whom Saint and his fellow missionaries had no language to communicate.

2. Are You Laying Down Your Rights?

In our efforts to reflect the heart of Jesus in the twenty-first century, Christians often conflate the idea of human rights with their personal rights. Throughout Scripture, we see that God's priority is to protect life whenever possible. In the Old Testament, God tells Moses that in some instances it's permissible for married couples to divorce—because that's a better option than murdering your spouse. In the New Testament, Jesus halts people from stoning an adulteress to death, despite Jewish law's allowance for such retribution and punishment. Protecting life makes sense. Throughout history, many Christians have fought valiantly for the abolition of slavery. Christians have also been vocal advocates for striking down laws allowing abortion in the United States and in other countries.

However, the gospel message becomes tainted when we begin imposing what we consider to be "our rights" on others. Instead of allowing Jesus' message of love and grace to ooze forth from the way we live, our efforts to assert our personal preferences and desires on others renders the gospel toothless. To a world that doesn't know Jesus, our reflection of Him is what they've got. When we make it our business to have our way in the public sphere, we offer a reflection of someone else entirely.

An unquenchable desire for rights by the Jews 2,000 years ago caused many of them to miss the Messiah. Jesus was born into a time of great complexity in Israel. With the Jews under the rule of the Romans, there was a diversity of social, political and religious ideas flowing through the culture. Some people wanted to oust the Romans by force—and made plenty of attempts, beginning with the first Jewish-Roman War from AD 66-73. Others, like the wealthy Sadducees, opted to preserve their power through compromise with the Romans. Then there were the Pharisees, who desired neither violence nor compromise, and the Essenes, who chose to ostracize themselves from society by living a more monastic life.

Among all these different ideas, there was one prevailing expectation of what the Messiah would do once He appeared: free God's people from the oppressive Roman rule. The real conflict between the religious leaders and Jesus began when Jesus asserted Himself as the Messiah, yet made it crystal clear that His mission entailed something completely different.

No, this was not what *their* Messiah was going to do. In their minds, Jesus had to be a phony. No amount of miracles or wisdom or convincing words would change the minds of religious leaders. *Their* Messiah was going to restore the Torah as the prevailing rule of law. *Their* Messiah was going to allow them to walk in freedom from other cultures and warring societies. *Their* Messiah was going to exalt God's chosen people above others. On top of everything else, they recognized that their positions of power and influence could be vanquished if people truly began to adhere to Jesus' teaching. The best course of action for the religious leaders was to brand Jesus as a heretic.

Those religious leaders were very disappointed when they saw their values eroded in the public sphere. They attempted to strong-arm people into going along with what they proclaimed as the truth, instead of presenting a path and inviting people to come alongside them. In short, they did the exact opposite of what Jesus did. Similarly, when we resort to strong-arming tactics today, it is to the detriment of the gospel, running counter to what Jesus taught and lived out.

It is a natural tendency to exert our desires for our culture, particularly if we feel like we are in a majority. We assume that since we live in a "Christian nation," we should be able to impose our values on others. We assume that it is our right to display whatever religious depictions and symbols we desire, even if doing so flies in the face of the law of the land. But is that the hill we need to die on?

When it comes to what Christians should spend their time fighting for, we often pick the wrong battles. It seems as though we are more concerned with our rights as churches and Christians than we are with the rights of those Jesus encouraged us to defend. Compassion is God's heart for the downtrodden. But the little things distract us—the meaningless issues in our society. In these cases, we end up supporting many unbelievers' perceptions that Christians are out of touch with reality (72 percent, according to the research in *UnChristian*) and insensitive to others (70 percent).[2] In no way do those characterizations fit Jesus. He was incredibly in touch with people and the culture, as well as sensitive to people and their needs. How do we want to reflect Jesus? What rights do we consider worth fighting for?

Shortly after winning the election to become Alabama's Supreme Court chief justice, prominent conservative judge Roy Moore decided to create a granite display for an area outside the courthouse. The display included the lyrics to "The Star Spangled Banner," quotations from some of the Founding Fathers, and excerpts from the Declaration of Independence. It was an impressive piece of artwork, commemorating many of the ideas from which our country derived its constitutional and legal framework. On August 1, 2001, Moore unveiled the granite slab—the text of which also happened to include the Ten Commandments—to the press in a photo opportunity that was akin to striking a match and hurling it into a bundle of sticks doused with gasoline.

Suddenly, a battle royal was on.

Moore likely had good intentions when he dreamed up this concept. He later told *The Atlantic* senior editor Joshua Green that he "wanted to establish the moral foundation of our law."[3] Instead, what he got was a bevy of court dates. Organizations like the American Civil Liberties Union and the Southern Poverty Law Center filed suits faster than a plague of swarming locusts could descend. Moore was ordered to remove the monument but chose to refuse, defending himself by testifying in front of the Alabama Court of the Judiciary that "to acknowledge God cannot be a violation of the Canons of Ethics. Without God there can be no ethics."[4]

In 2003, Moore ultimately lost his seat over his willful and public refusal to obey the law. Judge William Thompson, who presided over the hearing, said, "The chief justice placed himself above the law."[5]

It's an issue that strikes at the heart of Christian culture in America. We want to display our faith—and do it proudly. But whenever we are trying to develop a course of action to move forward in a situation such as this, we must ask ourselves: *Are the rights of the voiceless being taken away? Are there other ways to resolve this? Is this really necessary?* In trying to determine what course of action Jesus would take in a situation like this, we have to ask tough questions. In our politically charged culture, we can be quick to look past the complexities of an issue and act based on our emotions. "We have rights!" we scream. So we try to assert them. But sometimes we make too much of rights that are far beyond the bounds of basic human rights.

Lost in all the controversy swirling around Judge Moore was an often-neglected fact: The Ten Commandments were already displayed at the Alabama State Supreme Court. The display just wasn't grand or appropriate enough for God, in Judge Moore's opinion. He wanted something more.

There have been times in our country's history when civil disobedience has been appropriate—situations where standing up for the rights of the voiceless was necessary and important. Even today, there are issues, like abortion, where we still need to speak up for the rights of the voiceless. But where we can veer off course is when we instigate conflict for the sake of our *own* rights. Jesus provoked religious leaders, but only to reveal that their pious hearts were actually selfish or deviant. Their intentions in leading others in the name of God were not pure.

When we hold up an action to the light of the way that Jesus lived His life, we have to ask ourselves whether this is the way Jesus would spend His time? Did He attempt to force the public to swallow the gospel message—or did He simply offer it as hope for those who were truly seeking? Did He call us to make sure our culture knows how important the law is—or did He call us to make disciples of others?

It's easy for Christians to become distracted by endeavors that seem worthwhile, such as rallying to support the public display of the Ten Commandments. Of course we want to have such freedom because we believe it's a founding principle of this nation. But is that advancing the cause of Christ? Is that reflecting positively or poorly on Jesus? Would outsiders think more of us or less for getting embroiled in a protracted legal battle that began when we refused to obey the law of the land?

What's most important to remember is that God's law can be written on our hearts, whether or not we're allowed to inscribe it in granite. Defending our collective rights as a group of Christians is not what Jesus intended. Rather, Jesus calls His followers to stand up for the rights of others. He models what that looks like by reaching out to those on the fringes of society, healing the sick, freeing the oppressed, and serving those whom culture would deem to be below Him. Jesus laid down His rights, preferring others above Himself.

3. Are You Listening More Than You're Talking?

Most people enjoy talking about themselves—we like to tell our stories and hear our own voices. What most people *don't* enjoy is listening to others talk about themselves. Proverbs 18:2 says this: "A fool finds no pleasure in understanding but delights in airing his own opinions." Jesus took the time to ask questions and listen to people's answers. If we're serious about sharing our faith, we'll learn another upside-down Kingdom principle: Sharing our faith starts with listening to others share their hearts.

My (Jason's) friend Lori teaches a popular local Bible study for women and routinely talks about the issue of our rights as Christians. My wife regularly attends and shares with me all of Lori's wise teaching. The recaps I get are so good, I sometimes ponder wearing a wig and slipping into the back just to hear what Lori is teaching.

Lori once shared with me a powerful story that illustrates how important listening can be when it comes to sharing our faith. A young woman who began attending Lori's Bible study shared with Lori that she was concerned about her brother's state of salvation. Over a period of time, the woman had been visiting her brother in prison and sharing the gospel with him—and he didn't want to hear it anymore. Her friendship evangelism approach—which was more like pushy prison preaching—resulted in him telling her that he didn't want to see her anymore if all she was going to do was preach at him. Her attempt at love entailed regular beatings over the head with the Bible—and to no avail. So, the woman raised this concern with Lori.

"I told her that in her enthusiasm to share the good news of Christ, she was pushing him away," Lori said. "I told her to just go and love him by listening to him—and forget trying to share the gospel with him. Loving him *is* the gospel."

"But if I drive all that way"—an hour and a half each way— "I don't want to talk about the weather or what movie he saw on TV," the woman said.

"Well, true love lays down our rights, including what you feel is your right to say what you want to say about the Bible just because you drove all that way," Lori responded. "Just try it, like a science experiment, and see what happens."

What happened was that the woman became more relaxed and quit worrying about how she was going to make an argument that would convince her brother to become a Christian. She began to love on her brother during her regular visits by simply listening. Over time, her brother began to see that she truly cared for him. Then he dropped a bomb: He asked a deep spiritual question relating to salvation. For a year and a half, the woman visited her brother with no expectation of talking about the gospel—but got to anyway—before she eventually helped him begin his journey with Jesus. Instead of trying to change her brother's heart, she changed her own.

4. Are You Embracing Meekness?

Throughout Jesus' time on earth, He continually went against the grain. His upside-down Kingdom was, and is, something to behold—and something that needs to be completely bought into, or else its citizens will be ineffective at promoting it. Jesus calls His followers to resist the urge to demand their personal and collective rights and instead heed God's call to do what is right. In a word, Jesus calls us to be *meek*. But not even Jesus' closest disciples fully grasped what He meant right away.

> While he was still speaking, Judas, one of the Twelve, arrived. With him was a large crowd armed with swords and clubs, sent from the chief priests and the elders of the people. Now the betrayer had arranged a signal with them: "The one I kiss is the man; arrest him." Going at once to Jesus, Judas said, "Greetings, Rabbi!" and kissed him.
>
> Jesus replied, "Friend, do what you came for."
>
> Then the men stepped forward, seized Jesus and arrested him. With that, one of Jesus' companions reached for his sword, drew it out and struck the servant of the high priest, cutting off his ear.
>
> "Put your sword back in its place," Jesus said to him, "for all who draw the sword will die by the sword. Do you think I cannot call on my Father, and he will at once put at my disposal more than twelve legions of angels? But how then would the Scriptures be fulfilled that say it must happen in this way?" (Matt. 26:47-54).

In one powerful moment, Jesus embodied what it meant to be *meek* as His culture used the word. Perhaps it is because the words "meek" and "weak" sound similar in English that we think of a meek person as one who is feeble and humble—a doormat for others. But that's not the connotation this word had in Jesus' era.

The Greek word *praus* is actually a powerful word. It was regularly used to describe a wild horse that had been tamed and could be controlled by its master with the smallest of actions. A nudge to the left or right was all the horse needed. If a horse was capable of such obedience, it was designated as a warhorse—the kind you could trust in battle to face the heat of a fierce charge or attack. The horse's ability to keep all its power under control was an exceptional trait, one that earned it the most crucial of missions. It was tamed, yet still swift and commanding.

In the encounter in the Garden of Gethsemane, Jesus exhibited extraordinary meekness as just defined. He could have called twelve legions of angels to help Him escape the mob Judas had brought to seize Him—but He didn't. He withheld His power because He answered to the Father. Instead of fighting for His life, Jesus laid down His life—and He did it willingly, without a struggle. In doing so, Jesus completely represented the heart of God, who could have His way but chose not to. He never forces His love on anyone; He wants it to be a choice. He wants us to choose Him.

However, in our zeal to share the gospel and make a statement in the face of an opposing culture, we often do what Peter did—we whip out our swords and start swinging. We aren't concerned with the casualties or the outcome of our actions. No, we just want to make the point that we're still here and must be reckoned with. But Jesus dismisses such a wild, frivolous and uncontrolled act as something that does not exemplify His heart for the world. Are we willing to die by the same sword we wield when conflict arises? Jesus warns us that such a consequence will occur.

By healing the servant's severed ear, Jesus dispels the notion that making His name known and developing disciples is going to be a physical struggle. Instead, it will be a battle waged through spiritual warfare. Jesus categorically denies that violence is the route to take, and He lays down another path—a path that is much more difficult. It is the path of greatest resistance—fraught with fury and dangers placed in the way by those who wish to destroy the virtues of the Christian life in the public sphere. But such attacks only serve to increase the gospel's potency, as they have in China.

In the book *God Is Red*, Liao Yiwu describes his 2009 encounter with then-101-year-old Sister Zhang Yinxian in Dali, China. At age three, Sister Zhang became an orphan and was sent by her uncle to serve in a small monastery in Kunming. She later returned to Dali to live with her aunt. In the 1920s, the Catholic Church in Dali experienced incredible growth, swelling to more than 80,000 parishioners from various ethnic groups. The church expanded to accommodate all the growth—building a monastery, orphanage, and a larger church building. Sister Zhang became a nun and served in the church's orphanage, which housed more than 200 orphans by the 1940s. She worked in the kitchen, helping prepare meals for the children.

Then the Communist takeover commenced, and by 1952, soldiers had boarded up Sister Zhang's church. Mao Tse-tung exerted pressure through his government to get people to renounce the Catholic Church and say that it enslaved people. Eventually, the government seized the church's assets, leaving Sister Zhang without a home. For nearly 30 years, the church had been her home, but now she had to leave, along with her aunt and the church's bishop.

A few months later, local militia forced Sister Zhang and her aunt at gunpoint to another village. But before they left, a public denunciation meeting was held. At this meeting, the nuns, along with various other religious leaders from the community, faced angry villagers who shouted revolutionary slogans. In their new village, Sister Zhang and her aunt were tasked with physical labor, as local villagers were charged with supervising the reformation of their minds. For the next 31 years, Sister Zhang and her aunt worked in the field, growing vegetables to support themselves.

Sister Zhang related the story of how her aunt encountered one man who derided her as being a "lackey of the imperialists who exploited us," referring to the Catholic Church. That was how Mao Tse-tung had indoctrinated the people, painting the Catholic Church as something evil and self-seeking. As the man threatened to hit Sister Zhang's aunt, she said, "Slap me if you want. If you slap me on the left side of my face, I will give you the right side too."

In 1983, when the Communist party began allowing religion in the country under the government's auspices, Sister Zhang and her aunt reunited with the bishop to regain control of their previous church. A bureaucratic battle of the wills followed, with the pair of nuns—Sister Zhang at age 75 and her aunt nearing 90—holding a sit-in. They sat outside of a government building, praying and fasting for 28 days until they caught the attention of a government official. A few months later, they got their church back, although they received only a quarter of the original amount of property seized by the government. Eventually, the old bishop died, and the church got a new bishop. A new generation of nuns now runs the church.

At the end of Yiwu's interview with Sister Zhang, he asked her what she would like to do. She said, "I would like to continue to praise the Lord. I would like to get to make sure that our church gets back our land. I would like to continue."

Stories like Sister Zhang's fill the pages of *God Is Red*, telling story after story of people who endured great suffering for the sake of the gospel. These dear Christian brothers and sisters share stories unlike any western Christians generally experience in the modern era. They have reflected the heart of Jesus in powerful ways as they personified meekness. Instead of fighting for their rights, Sister Zhang and her aunt allowed themselves to be tamed by the Master, dutifully serving where they were called with the express purpose of one day returning to re-open the church and its school and orphanage.

5. Are You Putting Others First?

It is counterintuitive to consider taking a back seat to anyone these days. In our me-first society, we are saturated with messages about the way we should prefer ourselves over others. *Enough about you—what do you think about me?* We seek the spotlight—our 15 minutes of fame—and we do it with such dogged determination that we hardly have time to notice anyone else for our long glances in the mirror. But what do we see? Do we see a reflection of Jesus—one that is attractive to unbelievers who don't know Him?

The apostle Paul had this to say about how we should put others first:

> Let love be without hypocrisy. Abhor what is evil; cling to what is good. Be devoted to one another in brotherly love; give preference to one another in honor; not lagging behind in diligence, fervent in spirit, serving the Lord; rejoicing in hope, persevering in tribulation, devoted to prayer, contributing to

the needs of the saints, practicing hospitality (Rom. 12:9-13, *NASB*).

"Give preference to one another in honor." Paul offered this as a way to help us show that our love is genuine. When we prefer ourselves over others, we demonstrate that our love is conditional—perhaps even shallow or situational or rooted in convenience. But authentic love is much more than that. It looks at another and says, "You first." When this attitude takes hold in our lives, we begin to reflect the heart of Jesus in the way that He intended for us to reflect it.

But the change is not easy or natural. In fact, we need to tame our wild hearts, choosing to place others first. It's a life-long exercise that will yield bountiful fruit when executed correctly. Others stop seeing us and begin seeing Jesus. As John the Baptist put it, "He must increase, but I must decrease" (John 3:30, *ESV*).

We need to ground ourselves in the truth of God's Word. We can start by practicing with our loved ones.

"Honey, can you change Elijah's diaper?" came my (Jason's) wife's request from the other room. She was on the phone with someone, and our six-month-old son needed a new diaper.

I am not one of those dads who freaks out at the sight of a dirty diaper. By kid number three, if you're still uncomfortable with dirty diapers, you've got some major problems. Kids don't come out of the womb potty trained, and you just have to get used to it.

But this wasn't a routine diaper change request. The Georgia-Florida game was in the fourth quarter. *And Georgia was winning. Surely a dirty diaper could wait.* Leaving the living room where I was watching the game to change a diaper bordered on treason. Sometime after my academic advisor required me to sign off on my final transcript, I believe I also signed a piece of paper saying I would never miss the Georgia-Florida game. So, I wasn't exactly ready to leap into action.

An argument broke out in my head. This should have been a black-and-white issue. My wife asked me to help. The correct response was an immediate "yes." But I also saw this as a red-and-black issue, as in the colors of my alma mater. *Why did I need to do this now? Couldn't my wife just get off the phone or put the phone down so I could finish watching this thrilling fourth quarter? Why me? Why now?*

"Jason!"

Despite the ongoing tug-of-war in my head, I had yet to utter a word, entranced by Georgia's offense driving down the field for another score. I knew I had to make a decision to serve my wife and get my son out of a wet diaper or assert my imaginary right to watch college football on Saturday afternoons. *But it's my right to watch this football game!* Despite my desire to remain anchored to the couch, I knew there was no justifiable defense. I had to think about my son, who needed to be changed and cleaned—and could do nothing about it. I had to think about my wife, who was engaged in an important discussion on the phone. For a moment, I had resisted the call to prefer them. I was choosing to prefer myself and my football game. My precious football game. It was silly and I knew it. I had to change my attitude—demonstrate some authentic love—and do it quickly.

"Coming," I said, seriously wondering if my team would be able to score without me watching. Somehow, I made it back in time to witness my team's touchdown—and watched the rest of the victory with my son, who was happily sporting a fresh diaper. It was a small moment, but one that served as a reminder that I am not at the center of the universe—and that I will never have an excuse to put myself there. Inevitably, I will have an opportunity to place someone else's needs over my own. The more often I make that choice, the more clearly my life reflects the heart of the One who made the most unselfish choice in the history of the universe.

6. Are You Renewing Your Mind?

If we're going to accurately reflect the heart of Jesus, we need to experience a daily renewal of our minds. It's one thing to know that we need to be reading God's Word and let it penetrate our hearts; it's another thing to commit to it and allow the transformative work to occur. The apostle Paul explained how a renewed mind functions:

> I appeal to you therefore, brothers, by the mercies of God, to present your bodies as a living sacrifice, holy and acceptable to God, which is your spiritual worship. Do not be conformed to this world, but be transformed by the renewal of your mind, that by testing you may discern what is the will of God, what is good and acceptable and perfect (Rom. 12:1-2, *ESV*).

Transformation is an issue of the mind—a process of coming into a new worldview. It means no longer seeing the world the way everyone else does, but rather through the eyes of God. It's a Kingdom perspective, diametrically opposed to the old way of seeing things.

Transformation involves grasping God's perspective not only for the world but also for your own life. It is coming into the reality that your life isn't an accident, but rather perfectly designed and planned. It is the awareness that you were created for a purpose. This renewal is an inward work of the Holy Spirit—a healing work that encompasses the hope that the renewed believer will discover God's good, pleasing and perfect will for his or her life.

In Romans 12:9-18, Paul paints a picture of what a person with a renewed mind looks like: someone who loves others; hates what is wrong; honors others; works hard; serves God and others with joy; and is patient, prayerful and at peace. This is a powerful description of the way Jesus spent His time on earth. As such, it represents a well-trodden path that we must follow if we are to truly reflect Jesus' heart to the world.

7. Are You Living Out Isaiah 61?

When the Vineyard movement was first established as a group of like-hearted, like-minded ministries in the early 1980s, John Wimber, the Vineyard's primary founding leader, provided the bulk of the vision and direction. As I (Tri) became involved in the Vineyard, I learned that John's initial intention wasn't to build a church growth movement, but rather to lead and pastor a new church he and his wife, Carol, had planted in Yorba Linda, California. But God had a different plan for John, and soon the handful of other congregations in the Southern California area that called themselves "Vineyard" churches began to look to him for leadership. This forced John to articulate the passions God had placed in his heart.

In this context, John rendered down the priorities for what was to become the Vineyard movement into two words: *worship* and *compassion*. In John's own words: "When I first became involved with the Vineyard we didn't have a name for the work God was doing through us. Later God revealed that his purpose for raising us up could be summed up in two words: 'worship' and 'compassion.' God was calling us to be worshippers of God and rescuers of souls." He went on to say, "It took time to understand what compassion ministry entailed. Several years of intense study of the Gospels as a congregation helped clarify God's purpose for us in our context. We've been called by a compassionate God to minister compassion in his name to the world around us."[6]

John's study took him to Luke 4. In an article John wrote for *Reflections* magazine titled "The Ministry of Jesus and the Mission of the Church," he shared that the Isaiah 61 prophecy, as recorded in Luke 4:18-19, was a statement of the essence of Jesus' ministry on earth. As he put it, it was "Jesus' messianic manifesto." With this new awareness, John stated, "This passage revolutionized my understanding of Jesus' purpose on earth."[7] He realized then that Jesus' mission encompassed more than simply saving souls.

> And he came to Nazareth, where he had been brought up. And as was his custom, he went to the synagogue on the Sabbath day, and he stood up to read. And the scroll of the prophet Isaiah was given to him. He unrolled the scroll and found the place where it was written, "The Spirit of the Lord is upon me, because he has anointed me to proclaim good news to the poor. He has sent me to proclaim liberty to the captives and recovering of sight to the blind, to set at liberty those who are oppressed, to proclaim the year of the Lord's favor." And he rolled up the scroll and gave it back to the attendant and sat down. And the eyes of all in the synagogue were fixed on him. And he began to say to them, "Today this Scripture has been fulfilled in your hearing" (Luke 4:16-21, *ESV*).

John's point was simply this: If this was Jesus' job description, and if we as His followers have been commissioned to carry on His ministry, then this must be our job description as well, at least when it comes to this issue of compassion. John said, "Preaching the good news is all-encompassing. It's telling people about Jesus, and salvation, but it's also feeding the hungry. It's praying for the sick, and casting out demons."[8]

As I (Jason) was raised up as a believer in the Vineyard, this value of compassion ministry was ingrained into me when I was a young Christian and continued to grow in my heart through the years. Looking back now, with years of senior leadership experience under my belt, I realize my passion for justice ministry has come naturally. It flows from following God's words, spoken in Isaiah 61:8: "For I, the Lord, love justice."

Our church started a ministry called i-61, which is about fulfilling this commission to care for the broken, the oppressed, the captive and the extreme poor under the promised anointing of the Holy Spirit. It is an organized effort to train and send authentic disciples to those to whom Jesus referred as "the least of these." Through various ministries created in the church, we address issues such as world hunger, environmental decline, poor health and disease, illiteracy and lack of education, human injustice, spiritual bondage and internal chaos, and corrupt and immoral leadership. Each of those issues represents a place where God's presence is needed in a very real way—places where people are oppressed by governments or other forces. It's our desire to use this Isaiah 61 blueprint as a way to build a framework around the idea of Christlike compassion.

Go. Be.

Our faith is only as contagious as the extent to which we reflect Jesus. If we reflect Christ poorly, others will not be interested. Who would want to follow a Jesus who has such poor disciples? It's a legitimate question. That's why we need to be asking ourselves—as members of the Body of Christ—how we can lay to rest the perception of J.A.M.E.S. that nonbelievers have when they hear the word "Christian" and foster an image that is more consistent with the nature of Jesus.

It is our prayer that the things you have learned as you have read through the pages of this book will provide a pathway to discovering what the heart of Jesus looks like and how you can reflect Him in a way that makes the Lord we serve irresistible to a world in search of answers.

ENDNOTES

Introduction
1. David Kinnaman and Gabe Lyons, *UnChristian* (Grand Rapids, MI: Baker Books, 2007), pp. 69-70.
2. Ibid., p. 50.

Chapter 1: A Broken Heart for a Broken World
1. David E. Garland, *First Corinthians*, Baker Exegetical Commentary on the New Testament (Grand Rapids, MI: Baker Academic, 2003), p. 215.
2. Jerry Bridges, *Transforming Grace* (Colorado Springs, CO: NavPress, 2008), p. 208.

Chapter 2: The Verdict on Judgmental Christians
1. David Kinnaman and Gabe Lyons, *UnChristian* (Grand Rapids, MI: Baker Books, 2007), p. 182.
2. Ibid., p. 30.

Chapter 3: Every Head Bowed, Every Heart Opened
1. Tom Wright, *John for Everyone, Part Two* (London: Society for Promoting Christian Knowledge, 2004), pp. 153-154.
2. Jonathan Edwards, *A Treatise Concerning Religious Affections* (Whitefish, MT: Kessinger Publishing, 2004), pp. 279-280.
3. Francis Frangipane, "It's a Package Deal," Ministries of Francis Frangipane. http://frangipane.org/cgi-bin/gx.cgi/AppLogic+FTContentServer?GXHC_gx_session_id_FutureTenseContentServer=16267f2dd470a5c8&pagename=Fait hHighway/Globals/DisplayTextMessage&PROJECTPATH=10000/1000/728&se rmonid=textsermon_1178140280361&customerTypeLabel=Weekly&sermontitle =It%27s%20a%20Package%20Deal.

Chapter 4: How Kind Are You?
1. William Shakespeare, *The Merchant of Venice*, Act IV, Scene I, 184-187, quoted in *The Riverside Shakespeare* (Boston: Houghton Mifflin, 1974), p. 276.

Chapter 5: The Exclusive-Inclusive Club
1. Brennan Manning, *The Ragamuffin Gospel* (Sisters, OR: Multnomah Publishers, 2005), p. 52.

Chapter 6: The Heart of a Pharisee
1. Philip Yancey, *The Jesus I Never Knew* (Grand Rapids, MI: Zondervan, 1995), p. 144.
2. Andrew A. Bonar, *Memoir and Remains of the Rev. Robert Murray M'Cheyne* (Dundee, Scotland: William Middleton, 1852), p. 462.

Chapter 7: Carve Your Name on Hearts
1. Charles Spurgeon, cited in Larry J. Michael, *Spurgeon on Leadership* (Grand Rapids, MI: Kregel Publications, 2010), p. 85.
2. David Kinnaman and Gabe Lyons, *UnChristian* (Grand Rapids, MI: Baker Books, 2007), p. 28.
3. Joshua Green, "Roy and His Rock," *The Atlantic*, October 2005. http://www.theatlantic.com/magazine/print/2005/10/roy-and-his-rock/4264/ (accessed February 2012).

4. Kyle Wingfield, "Alabama Chief Justice Removed from Office," *The Associated Press*, November 13, 2003. http://www.al.com/specialreport/?111303moore.html (accessed February 2012).

5. "Alabama Chief Justice Roy Moore Ousted from Office," *PBS Online NewsHour*, November 13, 2003. http://www.pbs.org/newshour/updates/alajudge_11-13-03.html (accessed February 2012).

6. John Wimber, "The Ministry of Jesus and the Mission of the Church." http://trirobinson.org/wp-content/uploads/2010/03/Wimber-on-the-Purpose-of-the-Church-2.pdf.

7. Ibid.

8. Ibid.

AUTHOR CONTACT

AUTHOR CONTACT

Tri and Jason both appreciate feedback and enjoy engaging with readers about their books.

To contact Tri, email him at:
Tri.Robinson@VineyardBoise.org

or connect with him on Twitter at:
twitter.com/@tri_robinson

You can also visit Tri's website at:
www.TriRobinson.org.

To contact Jason, email him at:
Jason.Chatraw@gmail.com

or connect with him on Twitter at:
twitter.com/@jasonchatraw

You can also visit Jason's website at:
www.JasonChatraw.com.

OTHER TITLES
BY THE AUTHORS

Revolutionary Leadership
by Tri Robinson

Is your church growing? More importantly, is your church creating authentic followers of Jesus? In *Revolutionary Leadership*, author and pastor Tri Robinson shares his journey of planting a church that is serious about discipleship. Out of his desire to pastor a chuch that was intentional and successful at developing passionate followers of Jesus, Robinson discovered the concept of synergy and how its components can help revolutionize leadership within a church.

Small Footprint, Big Handprint
by Tri Robinson

The world is changing whether we like it or not. The question that begs to be answered is this: Will you sit by idly and watch it change for the worse or will you allow God to put you on the forefront of changing it for the better? *Small Footprint, Big Handprint* is your invitation to embark on a journey for the latter.